WORLD HISTORY
a visual factfinder

Simone Becker
Schönhauser Straße 23
1000 Berlin 41
Telefon 791 46 18

WORLD HISTORY
a visual factfinder

KEN HILLS

Kingfisher Books

Kingfisher Books, Grisewood and Dempsey Ltd,
Elsley House, 24–30 Great Titchfield Street,
London W1P 7AD

First published in 1993 by Kingfisher Books
10 9 8 7 6 5 4 3 2 1 (hardback)
10 9 8 7 6 5 4 3 2 1 (paperback)

British Library Cataloguing in Publication Data
A catalogue record for this book is available
from the British Library

ISBN 1 85697 073 6 [hardback]
ISBN 1 85697 042 6 [paperback]

Series Editor: Michèle Byam
Assistant Editor: Cynthia O'Neill
Series Designer: Ralph Pitchford
Designers: Shaun Barlow, Cathy Tincknell
Picture Research: Elaine Willis, Su Alexander

Additional help from
Martin Wilson, Hilary Bird
Sandra Begnor
Janet Woronkowicz

Typset by Southern Positives and Negatives (SPAN)
Lingfield, Surrey

Printed in Spain

CONTENTS

6
About this Factfinder

9
Introduction

EARLY CIVILIZATIONS

10
Discovering the Past

12
The Birth of Civilization

14
The Beginnings of Beliefs

16
The Greeks

18
The Romans

THE MIDDLE AGES

22
Raiders and Invaders

24
Christianity and Islam

26
The Crusades

28
War and Plague

THE MODERN WORLD

30
The Renaissance

32
Reformation and
Counter Reformation

34
American Civilizations

36
The Age of Discovery

38
The East: India, China and Japan

40
The Colonization of America

42
European Society in the 1600s

44
Africa and the Slave Trade

THE AGE OF KINGS

46
Kings and Commoners

48
The Age of Reason

50
European Settlement Overseas

THE AGE OF REVOLUTIONS

52
The American War of Independence

54
The French Revolution

56
Napoleon Bonaparte

THE AGE OF IMPERIALISM

58
The Industrial Revolution

60
The New Nationalism

62
The American Civil War

64
The Movement of Peoples

66
Society in the 1800s

68
The Colonial Age

THE TWO WORLD WARS

70
World War I

72
The Great Depression

74
World War II

THE POSTWAR WORLD

76
The Cold War

78
The World Transformed

80
Retreat from Empire

82
The New World Order

84
People in World History

86
Key Dates in World History

89
Index

About this Factfinder

This encyclopedic reference book gives essential facts and figures about the most important events and people in the history of the world from prehistoric times to the present age. Each topic is interpreted in a highly visual style with colour illustrations, maps and photographs that complement the text.

A timechart gives quick and easy reference to major historical events and personalities. There are also box features that summarize additional key facts.

Short text essays introduce key periods of world history, including ancient empires and civilizations, the Renaissance, the Age of Discovery and the two world wars.

Clear and colourful maps provide further reference on wars and revolutions, world exploration, individual countries' territorial gains and losses, and social changes.

The Age of Discovery

The European navigators of the 1400s and 1500s sailed in search of profit; their discoveries were by-products of their voyages. Fortunes were to be made from the trade in ivory, jewels, perfumes, fabrics, and spices (which hid the taste of rotting food in the days before refrigeration). Many of the early voyages had a disastrous effect on the native populations. Whole tribes were slaughtered in the search for riches or wiped out by European diseases. Not until the 1600s did some explorers seek knowledge rather than gain.

1271–1295	1492	1768–1779
Marco Polo's travels through Asia	Columbus lands in America	Cook explores and charts the southern Pacific

THE AMERICAS
In 1492 the Italian Christopher Columbus sailed across the Atlantic from Spain to find a shorter trade route to China and India. He landed instead on Hispaniola in the Bahamas. The islanders thought the Spaniards were gods. Columbus believed that the islands were part of Asia and christened them 'The Indies'. Further explorations revealed the islands were not part of Asia but a totally new continent.

Columbus and islanders from Hispaniola

▶ The early Spanish and Portuguese voyagers chose boats called caravels for distant expeditions. Columbus's favourite ship, the Nina, was a caravel. She made at least five voyages to the New World. A caravel could be sailed by a 24-man crew. It was 21 m long, 6.5 m wide and could carry a cargo of 60 tonnes. Caravels were all-purpose craft. They were as dependable in ocean storms as when manoeuvring in shallow water close to uncharted coasts.

Compass

Backstaff

Mariner's astrolabe

▲ The simple navigation instruments of the 1400s were not very accurate. The compass, first used by the Chinese in the 1100s, was used to keep the ship on course. The backstaff and astrolabe helped the captain find the height of a star or the Sun so that he could work out the ship's latitude; they were difficult to use in bad weather.

Spanish caravel

Marco Polo 1271–1275
Dias 1488
Da Gama 1497–1498
Vespucci 1499
Magellan 1519–1522
Columbus 1492
Ibn Battuta 1325–1355
Cabot 1497
Cook 1768–1779

▲ Marco Polo's tales of China's wealth inspired the search for new trade routes to the East. Dias and da Gama pioneered the way around Africa. Columbus and Vespucci went west and found the route blocked by an unknown continent. Magellan's expedition was the first to sail around the world.

▼ Europeans knew little about the South Pacific until the three scientific voyages of the English explorer Captain James Cook in the mid-1700s. He charted Australia's east coast, claiming it for Britain. He later visited New Zealand. Cook was killed in Hawaii while looking for the North West Passage around North America.

EXPLORER DATES OF MAJOR JOURNEY

EARLY EXPLORERS

Marco Polo (Italy, c.1254–c.1324): Wrote of his 17-year stay in China

Ibn Batuta (Morocco, c.1304–1369): Travelled in E. Africa, Arabia, China

Bartolomeu Dias (Port., d.1500): First European to round Cape of Good Hope

Christopher Columbus (Italy, 1451–1506): Made four voyages to Caribbean

Amerigo Vespucci (Italy, 1451–1512): Sailed to Caribbean and S America

Vasco da Gama (Port., c.1469–1524): Pioneered eastern sea route to India

John Cabot (Italy, 1461–1498): Sailed across North Atlantic to Canada

Ferdinand Magellan (Port., c.1480–1521): Led first expedition around world

FURTHER FACTS
- When Columbus landed on Hispaniola, about 300,000 Arawaks were living there. By 1548, European diseases, murder by the Spaniards and death from working as slaves had reduced the islanders to about 500.
- The continent of was named after an Italian Vespucci, an Italian who sailed with the several expedition to visit northern South America in 1499.

The Great Depression

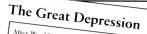

After World War I, democratic governments often seemed too weak and indecisive to handle the problems of peacetime, especially the economic crisis of the Depression. Both Italy and Germany became dictatorships under men who promised strong leadership and simple cures for their nation's woes. After a savage civil war, Franco emerged as Spain's leader. The USSR was governed by the tyrannical Joseph Stalin, who forced through a series of ruthless social policies in order to modernize his country.

January 1920
League of Nations' first meeting

January 1933
Hitler becomes German Chancellor

September 1939
German army invades Poland

PARTITION OF IRELAND

Ireland had been dominated by Britain since the 1100s. At Easter in 1916, British troops crushed a revolt in Dublin by Irish nationalists seeking independence. In 1918 the nationalists declared Ireland an independent state and the Anglo-Irish treaty of 1921, recognized the independence of southern Ireland as the Irish Free State. The six mainly Protestant counties of Ulster remained part of the UK.

◄ Dublin's post office was at the centre of the 1916 uprising.

Queue of unemployed in 1930s

Republican poster in Spanish Civil War

Hitler at Nazi rally

▲ As world trade declined in the 1930s millions were thrown out of work throughout the West. Banks collapsed, and people lost their savings. The unemployed rioted and everywhere the job queues lengthened. In America, the man-made calamity of the slump was made worse by a natural disaster. In 1934 and 1935, the Midwest was stricken by severe drought. Intensive farming had exhausted the soil and, as the crops died, there was nothing to bind it together. Gales arose and blew the soil away. Thousands of farmers and their families were forced off the land, their livelihoods ruined (left)

Voy a luchar por tu porvenir

▲ In 1936, officers of the Spanish army led by General Franco, rebelled against their government. The revolt swiftly developed into a civil war. Foreign states joined in. The fascist (extreme right-wing) powers, Germany and Italy, sent help to the army and its right-wing supporters. Communist Russia aided the government. By 1939 most of Spain had been overrun by the rebels and their leader General Franco was appointed head of state.

▲ In Europe the sacrifices of war had been followed by economic suffering. These difficult times provided opportunities for both the German Nazi Party under Adolf Hitler, and Benito Mussolini's Italian Fascist party. Both men came to power promising national recovery. Millions of their fellow-countrymen believed them. Soon both leaders were also seeking territorial expansion in Europe.

Russian tractors in 1930s

▲ Lenin died in 1924 and Joseph Stalin succeeded him as head of the USSR. Stalin set out to strip farmers of their land in order to reorganize farming in larger state-owned units called collectives. His orders were brutally carried out by the army and secret police. Villages were burnt and the villagers killed. Millions of people were transported to labour camps in Siberia.

MASS CULTURE

The new means of communication and travel which appeared between the wars started to break down the old barriers between classes and nations. The first worldwide form of mass culture was the movies. Film actors like the comedian Charlie Chaplin became international idols. In travel, faster aircraft brought the countries of the world closer together, and mass-produced cars increased private travel. In the 1930s, radio and the first television services brought information and entertainment to millions in their own homes.

Charlie Chaplin

Early wireless

Handley Page HP42 airliner, 1931

Model 'T' Ford

FURTHER FACTS

- **1919:** The German Nazi Party and the Italian Fascist Party were both founded.
- **1924:** The American Ford motor company produced its ten millionth car.
- **1935:** British publisher Allen Lane launched mass-market paperbacks with Penguin Books.
- **1939:** Pan American Airlines began the first regular trans-Atlantic air service.

73

Photographs provide a further source of visual information about the 20th century by showing significant world events such as the Great Depression of the 1930s.

Captions give comprehensive in-depth information on subjects such as the founding of the world's religions, famous battles, great empires, and important social changes.

Quick-reference data boxes provide essential facts and figures on the famous people, major events and historical movements that have shaped world history.

Detailed artworks showing scenes from each historical period and every major world civilization help to bring the story of humankind vividly to life.

After conquering most of India, the Mogul emperor Akbar tried to unite the many different peoples and religions.

WORLD HISTORY

*W*orld History is an illustrated guide that highlights the most important topics and trends in world history and the people and the circumstances that helped to shape them. The eight sections each cover a distinct period in the story of humankind, from the earliest evidence of human activity to the complex world of the 1990s. A chronology of world events and a collection of brief biographies of notable men and women supplement the main text.

Areas as diverse as the arts, science and technology, religion and the lives of people, both extraordinary and ordinary, are used to illuminate the major events of the past.
Together, the text and illustrations suggest some of the conclusions to be drawn from the study of history. Wars it seems rarely settle anything; rather they breed future conflict. History does not repeat itself, however, situations that are similar continually recur. Nor does *World History* assume that the history of the world is solely the story of Western nations. It shows that the achievements of the great civilizations of America and Africa were substantial and that certain Asian civilizations have been more advanced than those of Europe.

Ken Hills

EARLY CIVILIZATIONS

Discovering the Past

History is not just the study of past events and famous people; it is also the story of human ideas and advancement. Until the 1800s, knowledge of history depended almost entirely on the study of written records. In the past two hundred years the science of archaeology has revealed much about the people who lived before writing was invented, about 5000 years ago. Archaeologists can reconstruct the lives of prehistoric people by studying the objects, buildings or bones that they left behind. Through these reconstructions we can learn about the first humans, who lived by hunting animals, as well as about those hunters who learned to plant their food and so became the first farmers. We can also find out about the lives of people who lived in the early civilizations of Europe, Africa, China, the Americas, India and the Middle East.

RADIOCARBON DATING

The age of an ancient object can be fixed through radiocarbon dating. Living things absorb two kinds of carbon atoms – ordinary carbon, (carbon 12) and radio carbon, (carbon 14). When a plant or animal dies, the ratio of carbon 14 to carbon 12 decreases at a known rate. An archaeologist uses an instrument, a particle accelerator, to work out the age of an object by measuring its radiocarbon content.

▼ *Archaeologists find out about the lives of people who lived before the first written records were made (prehistory) by studying their bones, their tools and utensils and the remains of their buildings. A grid laid over the site is used to record exactly where each object was found.*

Pottery

Stone knife

▶ *The earliest humanlike creatures so far discovered are australopithecines (southern apes). Their remains have been found in southern and eastern Africa, where they lived between 4 million and 1 million years ago.*

THE CRADLES OF CIVILIZATION

Indus Valley

Tigris, Euphrates Valley

Huang He Valley

EGYPT
Nile Valley

INDIA

CHINA

▲ *The first centres of civilization grew up in the valleys of great rivers where there was plenty of water and soil was good for growing crops.*

◄ *The earliest farmers probably lived in the Middle East between 9000–8000 BC. In this village a ditch and fence prevent animals from escaping. Livestock graze in the main enclosure. They are fenced off from the houses around which vegetables are being grown.*

► *The earliest humans to look like modern people, lived over 130,000 years ago in small groups. They were continually on the move in search of food, fishing, hunting wild animals and gathering berries and roots.*

Flint arrowhead

▼ *We know the kind of animals prehistoric people hunted from paintings discovered on cave walls.*

11

The Birth of Civilization

About five thousand years ago, in four separate areas of the world – the Nile valley, the Tigris-Euphrates valley, the Indus valley and the Huang He valley – people in farming villages came together to establish towns. Later, they founded cities. The original farmers were compelled to work together in groups, to set up and manage the irrigation systems necessary to channel precious river water to the fields. This need for people to live together to control their environment may be the origin of civilization.

▼ *A huge desert to the west protected Egypt and enabled an early civilization to grow up there, free from attack by enemies.*

*c.*2371 BC–2316 BC Reign of Sargon, first ruler of Sumeria	1567 BC–1085 BC Ancient Egypt at height of its power	30 BC Romans conquer Egypt

▶ *Between 2630 and 1640 BC, the pharaohs (rulers) of Egypt built themselves gigantic tombs in the shape of pyramids made of blocks of stone.*

THE FIRST WRITING

The cities of Sumer in the region we now call the Middle East formed the world's first civilization. The Sumerians invented cuneiform writing, a series of signs and pictures. Their writing tells us how the Sumerians lived.

The Rosetta stone has enabled scholars to read hieroglyphics, the picture writing used by the ancient Egyptians. This is because the stone's message is also in ancient Greek, a language scholars already knew.

▼ *A labour force of 84,000 men working for 20 years was needed to construct Egypt's largest pyramid at Giza. The workers were peasants made to work on the pharaoh's building projects every year between the harvest and sowing the next crop.*

Desert

Worker's house

▶ *Criminals or prisoners of war built the tombs of the later pharaohs. Excavations show that they were housed in reasonable comfort. They lived with their families in cottages, consisting of an entrance hall, a living room, a kitchen and a bedroom. The houses were grouped in small settlements surrounded by high walls, patrolled by guards day and night.*

12

EGYPTIAN SHIPS

Pictures and models found in tombs show what the ships of ancient Egypt looked like. A picture dating from about 5000 BC shows a simple boat made of reeds sailing on the Nile. In 2613 BC the Pharaoh Snofru built a fleet of ships, like the one shown here. They could be rowed or sailed and were heavier than the craft that sailed on the Nile. The Egyptians used them for trading with the lands bordering the Mediterranean Sea.

Egyptian merchant ship, *c.*1500 BC

▼ *For nearly 4000 years from 4000 BC, the eastern Mediterranean was dominated by a succession of conquering nations: Babylonians, Assyrians and Persians. The most war-like were the Assyrians, whose fierce and ruthless soldiers made the Assyrian army the most effective the ancient world had yet seen.*

Covered raised road

Irrigated fields

Persian foot soldier

Babylonian archer

◄ *Every summer, the Nile overflowed onto the surrounding land. As Egypt has hardly any rain, farmers dug canals from the river to bring water to their fields after the floods had gone down. The arrival of floods ensured that the crops grew and fed the Egyptian people.*

— River Nile

— Temple

Assyrian war chariot and archer

FURTHER FACTS

• There are over 500 signs in cuneiform writing. It was taught in schools called 'tablet houses' after the clay tablets on which the signs were written.
• In ancient Egypt five holy days celebrated the chief gods; these were all rest days.

The Beginnings of Beliefs

Every human society has had some form of religion. That the earliest peoples believed in life after death is proved by the way corpses were buried with tools or pots for use in the afterlife. As the great civilizations developed in Asia, the Middle East, India and China, religious practices became more elaborate. Priests were appointed to ensure that religious ceremonies were properly observed. From 1500 BC to 500 BC many of the great religions of the world began to take shape within these civilizations.

*c.*1500–600 BC
Hindu religion develops in India

*c.*1200 BCs
Beginning of Jewish religion, which worships one god, Yahweh

▲ *Of the world's major religions, Hinduism and Buddhism started in India; Confucianism and Taoism in China. The Middle East was the birthplace of Judaism, and later of Christianity and Islam.*

▼ *A reconstruction of Solomon's temple. It is impossible to know exactly what it looked like as it was burnt down by the Babylonians in 586 BC.*

Solomon's temple

Workers constructing the temple

Bronze bowl for the temple water

▲ *The Hebrews or Israelites (later called the Jews) were 12 tribes who settled in Palestine. By the 900s BC Israel had become a wealthy nation; its king, Solomon, built a magnificent temple in Jerusalem as the centre of the Jewish religion.*

EASTERN RELIGIONS

Of the two great Indian religions only Hinduism has no founder. It combines the beliefs of the Aryan tribes who invaded India in about 1500 BC with the religion of the people they conquered. Buddhism, India's other great religion, was founded in the 6th century BC. Three centuries later, Emperor Asoka was converted to Buddhism. By the end of his reign, Buddhism had spread throughout India and beyond into Sri Lanka. The two ancient religions of China are Taoism and Confucianism. The story of the founding of Judaism is told in the book known to Jews as the Hebrew Bible and to Christians as the Old Testament.

Siva

▶ *Hinduism is the term used for the religious beliefs and practices of India. Among its most important gods is Siva, who is believed to be both creator and destroyer.*

▶ *Gautama, the Buddha, lived c.563–480 BC. He was a wealthy prince who gave up his life of luxury to become a poor wandering preacher in northern India.*

The Buddha

Lao-Tzu

◀ *Taoism came from ancient Chinese folk religions in about 500 BC. This statue is of a Taoist founder, Lao-Tzu, riding on a green ox.*

▶ *Confucius (c.551–c.479 BC) was a great Chinese philosopher or thinker. He was not a spiritual leader, but he taught the practical advantages of kindness, respect and personal effort.*

Confucius

FURTHER FACTS

● The followers of early religions worshipped many gods. The Jews were the first people to believe in one god, whom they called Yahweh.
● Taoism has more gods than most other religions; some of these gods are famous people, others are ancestors.
● Another major ancient religion is Shinto, the native religion of Japan; Shinto developed from early folk beliefs.

15

The Greeks

Ancient Greece was not one state with its own government. It was made up of many independent communities called 'city-states', who all shared the same language and culture. Between 800 and 400 BC the people of these miniature countries, particularly those of the most successful city, Athens, established many of the ideas that underlie Western civilization. But although democratic government started in Greece, only men could become citizens and vote – women (and slaves) were excluded.

THE MINOANS

The Minoans were traders who, between 2000 and 1100 BC, established the first major civilization in Europe on the island of Crete. *(Above)* A decorated Minoan vase and a frieze depicting a religious or magical rite that involved leaping over bulls.

*c.*3000–1100 BC	*c.*800–338 BC	323 BC
Minoan civilization	Golden age of Greek civilization	Alexander's death ends great age of Greece

▶ *About 1000 BC many of the original Greek cities had become overcrowded. By 500 BC, groups of citizens had left the mainland and settled in other parts of the Mediterranean.*

◀ *Well-armed Greek hoplites (foot-soldiers) were almost unbeatable on land. At sea, powerful Greek triremes rowed by 150 oarsmen overcame all opposition.*

ANCIENT GREECE AND ITS COLONIES c. 500 BC

GAUL

CORSICA

ITALY
Rome

SARDINIA

SICILY
Syracuse

Carthage

MACEDONIA

GREECE
Delphi · Athens
Olympia · Sparta

CRETE

EGYPT
Cyrene

Byzantium

ASIA MINOR

CYPRUS
RHODES
Sidon
Tyre

Alexandria

Trapezus
Sinope

ALEXANDER THE GREAT

Alexander, king of Macedon, was one of the greatest generals of all time. When he died in 323 BC, aged only 32, he left behind an empire that extended from Greece to India. In 333 BC at Issus *(below)*, Alexander won a great victory when his troops defeated a much larger Persian army led by the Persian king Darius *(right)*. By 330 BC Alexander had conquered all of the Persian empire.

EMPIRE OF ALEXANDER THE GREAT c. 500 BC

MACEDONIA
· Athens
CYPRUS · Issus
Mediterranean Sea
Alexandria
EGYPT
MESOPOTAMIA
PERSIA
Babylon
AFGHANISTAN

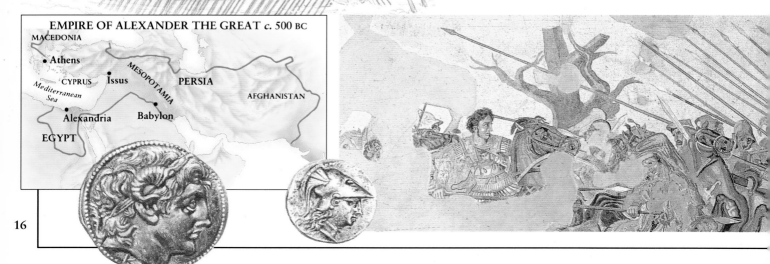

◄ The Greeks did not invent their alphabet. They adopted a set of signs used in Syria and modified them to form a simple alphabet of 24 letters.

► Greek plays were acted in open-air theatres. Some theatres seated over 10,000 people. Men wearing masks played all the parts.

● In about 1500 BC, a volcanic eruption blew apart the island of Santorini (now Thera). The subsequent tidal wave destroyed many of the Minoan cities on Crete, 96 km away.

● The first Olympic Games were held at Olympia in western Greece in 776 BC. They were repeated every four years, and they originally also included musical and literary competitions, as well as running and gymnastics.

▲ A bronze statue of a Spartan girl athlete. The city of Sparta was a powerful rival of Athens. Spartan women lived the freest lives of any women in ancient Greece.

► An 'acropolis' was a fortress on a hill where citizens took shelter in times of danger. The Acropolis in Athens is famous for its shrines and temples, such as the Parthenon.

► In Athens, all citizens over 30 served on juries. Each juror was given two bronze tokens. Tokens with a solid centre meant 'innocent'. Those with a hole meant 'guilty'.

► The Greeks told stories of their gods in which they behaved like ordinary people. On this decorated plate Hades, god of the underworld, drinks with his wife, the goddess Persephone.

17

The Rise of Rome

According to tradition, Rome was founded by Romulus and Remus in 753 BC. Until about 500 BC, Rome was one of several towns ruled by the kings of Etruria in the region now called Italy. After the Etruscans were overthrown the city of Rome became a republic. The Romans were a warlike people who sought to gain new territory. Their greatest rivals in southern Europe were the Carthaginians, whom they defeated in the three Punic Wars. By 44 BC the Romans controlled most of the Mediterranean lands.

*c.*500 BC	264 BC–146 BC	27 BC
Founding of Roman republic	Three Punic Wars against Carthage	Roman republic ends; empire begins under Augustus

▼ *In amphitheatres the Romans watched wild animals or gladiators fighting each other to the death.*

▲ *Legend says that Rome's founders, Romulus and Remus, were abandoned as babies but were found by a she-wolf who fed them on her milk.*

THE ROMAN CIRCUS

Rome's chariot-racing stadium, the Circus Maximus, was 550 m long by 180 m wide. The stands could hold up to 250,000 spectators; more than a quarter of the population of the city.

▼ *The Romans were greatly influenced by Greek drama and both plays and theatre were copied from the Greeks. In this mosaic from a house in Pompeii, Roman actors and musicians are preparing to perform in a Greek play.*

▼ *Most Roman shops were small. Jewellers, bakers, carpenters, shoe-makers, tanners and ironmongers made what they sold in workshops attached to their premises. In this smithy (left), the smith's tools are shown separately. Everyday objects such as keys, household lamps and coins (below) were all hand crafted.*

Key

Oil lamp

Coins

GLADIATORS
Gladiators were slaves
or criminals who were
trained in special
schools to fight each
other or wild animals in
the amphitheatres.

POMPEII
In AD 79 the
volcano Vesuvius
erupted, burying
the Roman port and resort town of Pompeii in
southern Italy. In 1748 the town was
rediscovered. Volcanic ash and cinders had
preserved the ruins and the shapes of the
bodies of citizens, who were unable to get
away in time. A baker *(above)* was found
beside the loaf of bread he had just baked.

HORSE RACES
Vast crowds flocked to
watch and bet on chariot
races. Charioteers raced
in teams wearing team
colours. Some racegoers
formed supporters clubs.

◄ *The Romans
built superb
roads throughout their
empire. The roads
were brilliantly
engineered across
marshes, tunnelled
under hills and
carved along the
sides of
mountains.*

► *Baths
were not
merely places
to wash in but were
centres where people
went to relax and meet
friends. Fresh water
was brought from the
hills to the towns by
aqueducts and pipes.*

▼ *Grand houses
were owned by rich
citizens. In the
country, they lived
with their servants in
villas on big estates.*

► *The Romans
worshipped a number
of gods and each of
their many temples
was dedicated to a
particular god or
goddess.*

▲ *The forum was originally the town
marketplace. Later it became a square
surrounded by buildings where business
was carried out.*

The Roman Empire

The empire founded by emperor Augustus in 27 BC lasted for nearly 500 years. At its greatest territorial extent, about AD 100, it stretched from Spain in the west to the Persian Gulf in the east. For two hundred years, the Roman empire was relatively peaceful. But the 3rd century AD saw the beginnings of turmoil as migrating tribes attacked the empire's eastern frontiers. Eventually, the empire was split into an Eastern empire with its capital in Constantinople, and a Western empire ruled from Rome.

27 BC–AD 14
Reign of Augustus, first Roman emperor

AD 395
Roman empire split in two by Theodosius

AD 476
Romulus Augustus, last emperor of Western empire deposed

▲ *The senate was the governing council of the Roman republic. Its members were retired government officials, most of whom came from wealthy families. Under Augustus the senate gradually lost its power.*

▼ *A legion was an infantry unit of the Roman army. It was made up of ordinary soldiers called legionaries commanded by officers (centurians). Standard bearers carried the legion's emblem. The legions' victories built the Roman empire.*

ROME'S ACHIEVEMENTS
Between about 27 BC and AD 200 the Roman empire was prosperous and peaceful. Travel was relatively quick and safe along the network of excellent roads which linked all parts of the empire.

A common coinage, language and legal system encouraged trade. Towns had fine public buildings and clean water. Outside the towns, irrigation and better tools led to more efficient farming methods.

▲ *The Roman empire was constantly under attack from invading tribes seeking land and plunder. Rome was finally overrun by Alaric, leader of the Visigoths, in AD 410.*

▶ *Roman legions were equipped with machines for attacking enemy strongholds. Catapults shot large arrows. The ballista was similar but fired stones.*

Centurion

Legionary

Standard bearer

ARMOUR AND WEAPONRY

By the 1st century AD, the Romans had replaced chain-mail with plate-armour. Flaps on the helmet gave better protection to the head. The shield had become rectangular and stronger. Javelins were weighted with lead. Swords remained short for stabbing the enemy in the close-quarter fighting at which the legions excelled.

▲ *The testudo or 'tortoise' was a formation tactic used by Roman soldiers attacking a fortress. The men held their shields overhead, in front and at the sides. This cover was strong enough to protect them from any missiles hurled down by the defenders.*

SPREAD OF CHRISTIANITY

Despite periods of persecution, Christianity spread through the Roman empire in the 2nd and 3rd centuries AD. Christians used secret symbols, such as a fish, to symbolize their religion. In AD 391 the emperor Theodosius made Christianity the state religion of the empire.

Early Christian fish symbol

▶ *By the 3rd century AD the Roman empire was in serious decline. Rival emperors struggled for power; in AD 238 alone no fewer than six reigned and were overthrown. Trade declined and corruption grew. On the frontiers, attacks by Germanic tribes increased. In AD 395 the Roman empire was divided into eastern and western parts. As the Eastern Byzantine empire thrived, Rome lost its power until it eventually disintegrated. The Western empire ended when a Germanic tribe deposed the last emperor.*

Western empire

Eastern empire

BRITAIN

FRANCE

ITALY
Rome

SPAIN

Constantinople
Black Sea

Athens
ASIA
MINOR

Carthage

Mediterranean Sea

EGYPT

Alexandria

Red Sea

▶ *The Emperor Constantine was converted to Christianity by a vision of a flaming cross. In AD 313 he issued an order allowing Christians to worship.*

THE MIDDLE AGES

Raiders and Invaders

The Middle Ages is the time in European history between ancient and modern times. The period is also known as the medieval period, from the Latin words *medium* (middle) and *aevum* (age). Early in the Middle Ages, western European civilization went through a period of upheaval and chaos as a succession of Germanic tribes surged through the former Roman empire. Meanwhile, the rise of Islam in the Near East gave

birth to a dynamic and warlike culture which gradually spread into southern and northern Europe. Elsewhere, powerful empires and highly-developed civilizations prospered in Asia and the Americas. By the late Middle Ages, the increased power of the European kings and the civilizing force of the Christian Church helped Europe recover from centuries of invasion, lawlessness and economic breakdown.

1066	1218–1224
William of Normandy conquers England	Genghis Khan's Mongols reach southeast Europe

▲ The Vikings were traders and warriors from Scandinavia who raided, and later settled, in parts of northern Europe between the 9th and 11th centuries.

Thor

Odin

◀ The Vikings believed in many gods, the most important of whom was Odin. Odin's son Thor was the god of thunder and war. Thursday (Thor's day) is named after him.

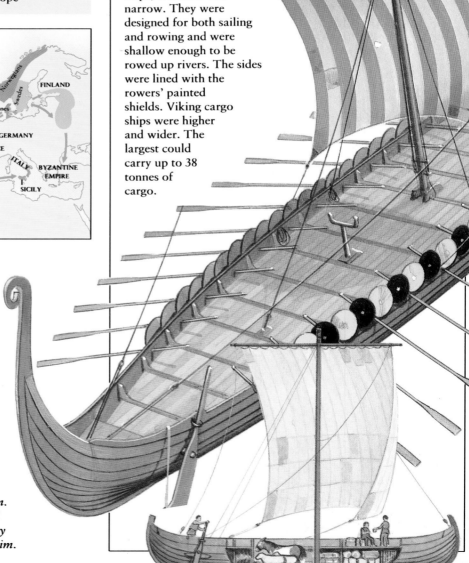

VIKING BOATS
Viking longships, or war ships, were low and narrow. They were designed for both sailing and rowing and were shallow enough to be rowed up rivers. The sides were lined with the rowers' painted shields. Viking cargo ships were higher and wider. The largest could carry up to 38 tonnes of cargo.

◀ *In the 1100s, tribes of nomadic peoples called Mongols, living in central Asia, united under a great warrior, Genghis Khan. The Mongols were to conquer a vast empire that stretched over China, and India, the Near East and into parts of Europe.*

▶ *There are many romantic stories about the British king, Arthur, his court at Camelot and the knights of the Round Table. There may be some truth in the legends. One early chronicle tells of a leader named Arthur who led the British against Saxon invaders in the 800s.*

Arthur and the knights of the Round Table

THE DOMESDAY BOOK

In 1085, William the Conqueror decided to find out who owned land and property and how much tax they should pay on it. His officials toured England recording the names of landowners, their holdings and how much their possessions were worth. The survey was called the Domesday Book.

THE NORMAN CONQUEST

The Normans were descended from Vikings who had settled in northern France. In 1066 their leader, Duke William, invaded England to seize the throne from King Harold. The English were routed at the battle of Hastings and William became king.

▼ *The Bayeux Tapestry is a gigantic strip-cartoon recording the Norman conquest of England. It was woven on the orders of Bishop Odo, half-brother of William the Conqueror. The section shown depicts Harold's death in the battle of Hastings.*

After his successful invasion, William the Conqueror consolidated his rule by crushing any revolts by English rebels

Christianity and Islam

Christianity originated in Palestine, Islam arose in Arabia; both regions of the Middle East. Christianity grew out of Judaism, the religion of the Jews, in the 1st century AD. Six centuries later, the prophet Muhammad preached to the Arab people that a single god, Allah, should replace the many gods they had worshipped before. Both faiths spread rapidly. Christianity became the dominant religion of Europe, but was in peril of being overwhelmed by Arab armies until an Arab invasion was halted in France in 732.

▼ *During the early Middle Ages people who believed they were called to devote their lives to God, began the practice of living in private communities. They did not mix with the rest of society. Women entered convents as nuns. Men became monks and lived in monasteries.*

Illumination by monks in medieval book

*c.*6 BC–*c.*AD 30	*c.*570–*c.*632	732
Life of Jesus Christ, central figure of Christian religion	Life of Muhammad, founder of Islamic faith	Battle of Poitiers halts Arab advance in Europe

▲ *Monasteries fed the needy and provided rest and food for travellers. Food was grown by the monks and cooked in the monastery's bakery, kitchens and brewhouse.*

A MONK'S DAY
2.30 a.m. Get up
3.00 a.m. Prayers
6.00 a.m. Prayers
7.00 a.m. Study
8.00 a.m. Prayers
9.00 a.m. Meeting
10.00 a.m. Work
12.00 a.m. Communion Service
2.00 p.m. Dinner
3.00 p.m. Recreation or study
4.00 p.m. Evensong
5.30 p.m. Supper
7.00 p.m. Prayers
8.00 p.m. Bed

▲ *The monastic movement split into different groups or 'orders', following different ways of life. The Cistercian order emphasized prayer, study and physical labour. In the Middle Ages they were known as superb farmers.*

▲ *When a monk fell sick or became too old to work, he was moved to the infirmary. Many orders of monks and nuns also cared for local old and sick people.*

24

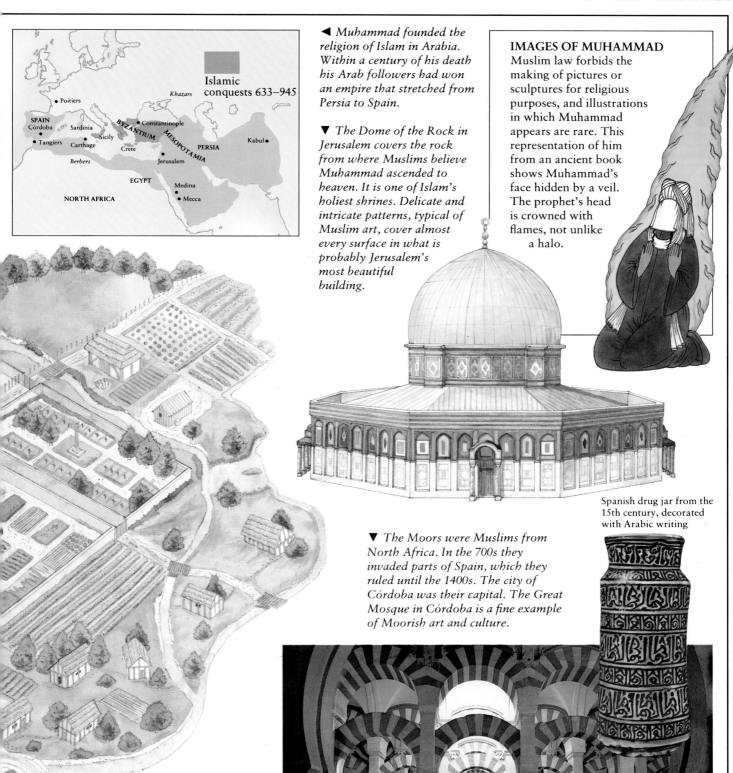

Islamic conquests 633–945

◀ *Muhammad founded the religion of Islam in Arabia. Within a century of his death his Arab followers had won an empire that stretched from Persia to Spain.*

▼ *The Dome of the Rock in Jerusalem covers the rock from where Muslims believe Muhammad ascended to heaven. It is one of Islam's holiest shrines. Delicate and intricate patterns, typical of Muslim art, cover almost every surface in what is probably Jerusalem's most beautiful building.*

IMAGES OF MUHAMMAD
Muslim law forbids the making of pictures or sculptures for religious purposes, and illustrations in which Muhammad appears are rare. This representation of him from an ancient book shows Muhammad's face hidden by a veil. The prophet's head is crowned with flames, not unlike a halo.

Spanish drug jar from the 15th century, decorated with Arabic writing

▼ *The Moors were Muslims from North Africa. In the 700s they invaded parts of Spain, which they ruled until the 1400s. The city of Córdoba was their capital. The Great Mosque in Córdoba is a fine example of Moorish art and culture.*

▲ *A monastery was often founded by a great landowner who then became its patron. The initial foundation included land around the monastery for gardens, orchards and the monastery's own farm. The patron might also give the monks the rights to build a mill, to catch fish in nearby rivers, and to receive gifts of food and produce from people who lived in nearby villages or towns.*

25

The Crusades

During the Middle Ages, many Christian pilgrims from Europe travelled to Palestine to worship at places associated with the life of Jesus Christ. In 1071 a Muslim people, the Seljuk Turks, conquered Palestine and brought these pilgrimages to an end. When Pope Urban II summoned European Christians to take up arms against the Muslims, thousands of knights and ordinary soldiers answered his call. For two centuries Christian armies strove to regain Palestine in wars called the Crusades.

1095–1099	1187	1217–1221
First Crusade captures Jerusalem. Four Christian kingdoms set up in Holy Land	Saladin, Sultan of Egypt, re-captures Jerusalem	The Fifth and last major Crusade

▼ *During the Crusades Muslims were called 'Saracens' by the Christians. The Saracens were superb warriors on horseback.*

▼ *During the Third Crusade Richard I of England won a major victory when his troops captured the Saracen fortress of Acre and defeated the army of the Muslim leader Saladin at Arsuf. This victory earned Richard the name of 'Lion-Heart'. Fighting in the Holy Lands or France, Richard seldom visited England. He is buried next to his mother, Queen Eleanor, at Fontrevault in France.*

▶ *Among the most feared Christian warriors were the Knights Templars. They were members of a religious military order who chose to serve God by fighting rather than through prayer.*

▲ *The Crusaders built castles to defend the lands they conquered. The largest and strongest Crusader castle was Krak des Chevaliers. It was built by the Knights Hospitalers (a military religious order) and lies in the desert of what is now Syria on a hilltop 750 m high. During the Crusades it was garrisoned by up to 2000 men. It held out against many attacks but finally fell to the Saracens in 1271 when the defenders were starved into surrender after a year's siege.*

Crusader castle of Krak des Chevaliers

THE ROUTES OF THE CRUSADES

First Crusade 1095–1099

Second Crusade 1147–1149

Third Crusade 1189–1192

HOLY ROMAN EMPIRE

Ratisbon
Vienna
Milan
Venice
Belgrade
Marseilles
Genoa
Rome
Adrianople
Durazzo
Constantinople
SELJUK TURKS
Lisbon
Cadiz
Jebel Tarik (Gibraltar)
Crete
Antioch
Tripoli
Acre
Jerusalem

◀ *Pilgrimages are journeys to holy places. The men and women who went on pilgrimages to the Holy Land often brought back a palm tree branch to lay on the altar of their church at home.*

▲ *Apart from the major Crusades, expeditions from countries as far away as Norway went to fight in the Holy Land.*

FURTHER FACTS

The capture of Jerusalem made the First Crusade (1095–1099) the most successful Crusade for the Christians. In 1187 Muslim armies took Jerusalem. and the Christians never recaptured it. The last Christian stronghold at Acre in Palestine fell to the Muslims in 1291.

◀ *In 1212 thousands of children from France and Germany joined a Crusade. They were inspired by a French boy, Stephen, and a German boy, Nicholas. Neither group reached the Holy Land. Many died of hunger or disease. Some were sold as slaves.*

CHIVALRY, HERALDRY AND TOURNAMENTS

The ideal knight was brave in battle, loyal to his lord and protected women. These rules of behaviour were known as 'chivalry'. Fully-armed knights displayed a sign on their shields or on their surcoat in order to be recognized in battle. During the 1100s each design or 'coat of arms' became the property of a particular family, a system known as 'heraldry'. Knights fought mock battles called 'jousts' in tournaments (*right*). They used blunted weapons and wore special armour. Each joust started with two knights charging each other with lances.

Jousting armour

War and Plague

The 1300s and 1400s were a disastrous period for Europe. The Hundred Years' War, fought when England tried to gain lands in France, was a calamity with parts of France laid waste by armies. In the mid-1300s, rich and poor alike died in the plague, known as the Black Death. Many peasants survived only to die of starvation as crops remained unpicked. About 25 million people may have died. Disorder became widespread. In France, Italy and England peasant revolts were crushed by the authorities.

1337–1453	1347–1353	1431
The Hundred Years' War	The Black Death rages in Europe	English burn Joan of Arc as a witch

Longbowman

Crossbowmen

▲ Bows and arrows were key weapons of the Middle Ages. Crossbows needed less strength to fire than longbows but were slower. The English longbowmen won famous victories at Crécy and Agincourt against far stronger French armies.

▼ In the 1300s the thick walls of a besieged castle could often withstand siege weapons. In this siege of a French town the English are using early cannons. By the mid-1400s cannons had improved; it was the increased fire power of the French artillery that helped them win the final battles of the war.

▼ As the the Hundred Years' War was being fought in Europe, a Mongol warrior Timur (or Tamerlane), who claimed to be a descendent of Genghis Khan, was building an Asian empire. Between 1379 and 1402, Timur swept south from his base at Samarkand (where he is shown being entertained) to invade Persia, India and Turkey.

▼ Inspired by mysterious 'voices', a French peasant girl, Joan of Arc, persuaded the French heir to throne, Charles, to give her troops to fight the English. In 1429 the army she led saved the city of Orléans from an English siege. It was the turning point of the Hundred Years' War. Later that year Joan stood beside Charles as he was crowned king at Rheims; by 1453 England had lost all its conquests except the port of Calais. Joan herself was captured and executed by the English. She was made a saint in 1920.

Route of plague from Asia

ENGLAND AND SCOTLAND 1348

SCANDINAVIA 1349

NORTH RUSSIA 1349

FRANCE 1347

SOUTH RUSSIA 1345

From Asia

ITALY 1347

SPAIN 1348

OTTOMAN EMPIRE 1347

SICILY 1347

◄ *The Black Death came to Europe from Asia in 1347. It began in Italy, spreading like wildfire to the rest of the continent.*

▼ *The Black Death was bubonic plague, a type of plague carried by the fleas living on black rats. The name came from a victim's black swollen lymph nodes; the disease was usually fatal.*

Black rat

THE BLACK DEATH
The Black Death was only one of the disasters to afflict Europe in the 14th century. Several bad summers and poor harvests brought starvation to many regions. Death became a frequent and familiar part of everyday life. Artists of the time depicted death in many forms, including a skeleton riding a horse.

◄ *People of the Middle Ages did not understand that disease thrives in dirt. It was usual to tip household rubbish onto the street and woe betide any unwary passer-by!*

FURTHER FACTS

● Although the Black Death killed between one quarter and one-third of Europe's population, parts of Poland, Italy, Bohemia and France escaped altogether. Less terrible epidemics continued for three centuries.

● At the time, people believed that cats and dogs spread the Black Death – so they killed them. As a result the true carriers, black rats, only increased.

◄ *At night plague carts were loaded with corpses to be taken away for burial. People in towns and communities such as monasteries suffered particularly badly from the plague since close-packed houses were ideal breeding grounds for the disease-carrying rats and fleas.*

THE MODERN WORLD

The Renaissance

The 1400s and 1500s saw a period of new learning – the Renaissance – that fundamentally changed the attitudes and ideas of educated people. This renewed scholarship and the questioning of established ideas which it fostered, marks the beginning of the modern world. News of advances in philosophy, arts and the sciences spread rapidly thanks to the development of the printed book. The new ideas also gave impetus to the Reformation – a movement that led to the division of western Christendom in the 1500s. An improved understanding of the Earth's geography encouraged Europe's seafarers and travellers to pioneer new routes in search of trade. At first European expansion hardly touched the empires of Asia but the civilizations of the Americas soon fell victim to the greed of the European invaders.

1300s	1400s–1600s	1400s–1700s
Birth of the Renaissance in Italy	Renaissance spreads from Italy to rest of western Europe	Florence ruled by the Medici family

▲ Italy in the late 1300s was the birthplace of the Renaissance. The development of printing in Europe in the 1450s helped to spread the Renaissance to other countries.

▶ A French nobleman travelling in Italy was impressed by the new architecture. Back in France he hired an Italian architect to build him this chateau in the same style. All over Europe, people were fascinated by the ideas and designs of the Italian Renaissance and copied them in their own countries.

▶ The new learning gave birth to humanism, a new way of thinking about human beings and their place in the universe. Humanists like the Dutch philosopher Erasmus rejected the belief that all actions are directed by God, in favour of the idea that people are responsible for their own lives.

French chateau built in Renaissance style

Merchant and his wife in Renaissance Italy

PATRONAGE BY POWERFUL FAMILIES

During the Renaissance, many great works of art and architecture were made possible by the patronage of rich families. In Florence the Medici, a family of merchants and bankers, were generous patrons of the arts. In Venice, the painter Vittore Carpaccio was commissioned by wealthy patrons to paint the townscapes for which he is celebrated (*left*: 'The Arrival of the Ambassadors' by Carpaccio).

▼ *The great cities of the Italian Renaissance such as Rome, Venice, Siena and Florence (shown here), were governed as independent states. The powerful families who ruled them had become rich from banking, as well as from trading in Asia and Europe.*

▼ *Although people had used devices to tell the time for thousands of years, the first spring-driven clocks with a dial and hour hand, were not developed until the 1400s.*

Early portable French clock (with its cover) from mid 1500s

◀ *The greatest thinkers of the Renaissance often anticipated future ideas. This sketch of a flying machine is by Leonardo da Vinci (1452–1519).*

▶ *The German Johannes Gutenberg introduced printing from moveable type into Europe in the 1450s. Books at once became relatively cheap and enabled the ideas of the Italian Renaissance to spread through the rest of Europe.*

THE RENAISSANCE IN EUROPE

ITALY: Brunelleschi (1377–1446), architect; Michelangelo (1475–1564), artist, architect; Galileo (1564–1642), astronomer	
FRANCE: Ronsard (1524–1585), poet; Rabelais (*c.*1494–*c.*1553), writer; Clouet (*c.*1485–1541), painter	
GERMANY: Gutenberg (*c.*1400–1468), printer; Dürer (1471–1528), painter; Holbein (*c.*1497–1543), painter	
SPAIN: Great age of Spanish exploration (*c.*1450–*c.*1550); El Greco (1541–1614), painter; Seville Cathedral (1517)	
HOLLAND/BELGIUM: Erasmus (*c.*1469–1536), philosoper; Bruegel (*c.*1525–1569), painter	
ENGLAND: Caxton (*c.*1421–*c.*1491), printer; More (1478–1535), scholar; Raleigh (*c.*1552–1618), poet, statesman	

Reformation and Counter Reformation

During the Middle Ages, Christians of western Europe belonged to a single Church, whose centre was in Rome with the Pope at its head. The Reformation of the 1500s started out as an attempt to reform the Church. It grew into a movement which gave birth to a variety of Protestant Churches and led to a permanent split in the Christian community. The Counter Reformation was the attempt by the Roman Catholic Church to reform itself and win back the loyalty of those who had left it.

Protestant

Roman Catholic

Roman Catholic and Protestant

1517
Luther's criticisms begin the Reformation

1536
John Calvin founds Protestant centre in Geneva

1545–1563
The Council of Trent establishes the Counter Reformation

◀ *In 1517 Martin Luther, a German monk and lecturer, nailed a list of 95 theses (statements) to the church door at Wittenberg. The theses challenged the authority of the Pope, who excommunicated Luther in 1521. His followers became known as 'Protestants' because they protested against the teachings of the Roman Catholic Church.*

▶ *For nearly 40 years Europe suffered from a series of religious wars. England, Holland and some German states fought on the Protestant side, while France and Spain supported the Roman Catholic cause. Massacres and the execution of dissenters occurred in several countries. In England many Catholics were executed in 1537, after an uprising during Henry VIII's reign.*

St Bartholomew's Day Massacre

▶ *Years of religious conflict between Catholics and Protestants followed the Reformation. The Catholic authorities burned Protestants to death for heresy. Protestants executed Catholics, sometimes with atrocious cruelty. On St Bartholomew's Day 1572, Catholic mobs in Paris killed about 3000 French Protestants.*

◀ *The Reformation split Europe. The north became mainly Protestant, while southern countries remained faithful to the Church of Rome.*

◀ *The Spanish Inquisition was set up in 1478 to arrest and punish those who did not follow the Christian faith. Its first victims were Muslims and Jews. After the Reformation, it attacked all forms of Protestantism. The Inquisition executed those it found guilty in great public spectacles called* auto-da-fés.

HENRY'S BREAK WITH ROME

In 1525 the Pope refused to let the English king, Henry VIII, have a divorce from his wife, Catherine of Aragon, so that he could marry Anne Boleyn. In order to legalize the divorce he wanted, Henry decided to take personal control of religion in England. By threats and persuasion he caused the English Parliament to pass an Act breaking all ties with the Pope in Rome. Henry then became absolute head of the Church in England.

Henry VIII and Anne Boleyn

▼ *In 1588, the English fleet defeated a large Spanish fleet, the Armada, sent by Philip II to overthrow the Protestant Elizabeth I and re-establish the Catholic faith. The Armada was defeated as much by bad weather as by the English, and only half the fleet returned to Spain. This victory helped establish the English as a major world seapower.*

Damaged Spanish galleon after the defeat of the Spanish Armada

Queen Elizabeth I

FURTHER FACTS

• In Martin Luther's time nailing theses to a church door was the recognized way of starting a debate.
• Luther's ideas were developed by a French Protestant, John Calvin, who was exiled in Geneva. Calvin's teachings were followed by Protestants in Europe and the Puritans, who later settled in America.
• The Council of Trent of 1545 began the Counter Reform movement which revived and reorganized the Catholic Church.

American Civilizations

American Indians, or Native Americans, were the first people to live in the Americas. They came to America from Asia over 20,000 years ago and developed many different lifestyles. When the Spanish arrived in Central America in the 1500s, they marvelled at the civilizations of the Aztecs and the Incas. They found wealthy, well-ordered cities, connected by good road systems. Far to the north, in what is now North America, people usually lived as hunters and farmers in small villages or as bands of nomadic hunters.

◀ *Between 300–900 the Mayans of Central America became an advanced civilization. They built massive pyramids, temples and other structures and were the only ancient American people to develop writing and an accurate calendar.*

c.300–c.900	1400s	c.1570
Mayan civilization in Central America	Aztec civilization at its height	The Mohawk join Iroquois League

Aztec sacrificial knife

Mayan temple

▲ *A warrior-tribe, the Aztecs, dominated Central America in the 1400s. Every night, priests ripped out the hearts of 100 human beings with a sacrificial knife to please their god of war. The Incas ruled an empire in Peru, South America. By the 1500s their civilization was at its peak, with great cities and beautiful works of art (below).*

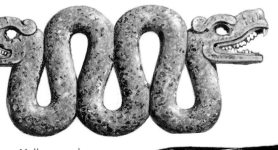

Hollow wooden snake covered in turquoise

Inca silver llama

Anasazi pueblos

▶ *The Anasazi were Native Americans who lived in what is now the southwestern United States. They built villages called pueblos, where houses were joined together to form a single, large building. The Anasazi abandoned their pueblos soon after 1200, when the local climate became too dry to grow crops.*

mahawk

Totem pole

◄ *Native Americans of northwest America erected carved totem poles either as memorials to their dead or as family records. Bows and arrows were a common weapon. The tribes of western North America developed hand axes called tomahawks.*

Bow and rrows

Sioux tepee

Iroquois man and woman

△ *The Iroquois were a group of hunting tribes: the Mohawk, Oneida, Seneca, Onondaga and Cayuga. They lived in the area that is now New York State.*

Northwest Coast

ESKIMO LANDS

Far North

Plains

Eastern Woodlands

Southwest

California-Intermountain

Middle American

Caribbean

Tropical Forest

Andes

Marginal

CULTURE AREAS OF NATIVE AMERICAN TRIBES

▲ *The major ancient American civilizations developed in completely separate parts of the Americas over several centuries.*

▲ *The Sioux tribes followed the buffalo herds as they migrated across the North American Plains. Sioux shelters (tepees) were made of buffalo skins.*

Mohawk village

▲ *Mohawk families lived in longhouses. Their villages were surrounded by a ditch and a stockade for protection. Mohawk women grew food in plots around the houses. The men hunted deer for meat and skins. The victorious colonists destroyed the Mohawk's villages in the 1700s because they had sided with the British in the War of Independence.*

35

The Age of Discovery

The European navigators of the 1400s and 1500s sailed in search of profit; their discoveries were by-products of their voyages. Fortunes were to be made from the trade in ivory, jewels, perfumes, fabrics, and spices (which hid the taste of rotting food in the days before refrigeration). Many of the early voyages had a disastrous effect on the native populations. Whole tribes were slaughtered in the search for riches or wiped out by European diseases. Not until the 1600s did some explorers seek knowledge rather than gain.

1271–1295 Marco Polo's travels through Asia	**1492** Columbus lands in America	**1768–1779** Cook explores and charts the southern Pacific

THE AMERICAS
In 1492 the Italian Christopher Columbus sailed across the Atlantic from Spain to find a shorter trade route to China and India. He landed instead on Hispaniola in the Bahamas. The islanders thought the Spaniards were gods. Columbus believed that the islands were part of Asia and christened them 'The Indies'. Further explorations revealed the islands were not part of Asia but a totally new continent.

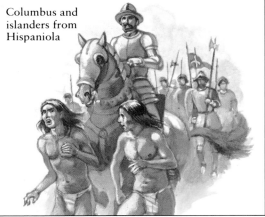

Columbus and islanders from Hispaniola

Compass

Backstaff

Mariner's astrolabe

▲ *The simple navigation instruments of the 1400s were not very accurate. The compass, first used by the Chinese in the 1100s, was used to keep the ship on* course. *The backstaff and astrolabe helped the captain find the height of a star or the Sun so that he could work out the ship's latitude; they were difficult to use in bad weather.*

▶ *The early Spanish and Portuguese voyagers chose boats called caravels for distant expeditions. Columbus's favourite ship, the* Niña, *was a caravel. She made at least five voyages to the New World. A caravel could be sailed by a 24-man crew. It was 21 m long, 6.5 m wide and could carry a cargo of 60 tonnes. Caravels were all-purpose craft. They were as dependable in ocean storms as when manoeuvring in shallow water close to uncharted coasts.*

Spanish caravel

THE AGE OF DISCOVERY

EXPLORERS/DATES OF MAJOR JOURNIES

GREENLAND
RUSSIA
EUROPE
CHINA
NORTH AMERICA
INDIA
KHMER EMPIRE
AFRICA
SOUTH AMERICA
AUSTRALIA
NEW ZEALAND

Marco Polo 1271–1275

Dias 1488

Da Gama 1497–1498

Vespucci 1499

Magellan 1519–1522

Columbus 1492

Ibn Battuta 1325–1355

Cabot 1497

Cook 1768–1771

▲ *Marco Polo's tales of China's wealth inspired the search for new trade routes to the East. Dias and da Gama pioneered the way around Africa. Columbus and Vespucci went west and found the route blocked by an unknown continent. Magellan's expedition was the first to sail round the world.*

▼ *Europeans knew little about the South Pacific until the three scientific voyages of the English explorer Captain James Cook in the mid-1700s. He charted Australia's east coast, claiming it for Britain. He later visited New Zealand. Cook was killed in Hawaii while looking for the Northwest Passage around North America.*

EARLY EXPLORERS

Marco Polo (Italy, *c*.1254–*c*.1324): Wrote of his 17-year stay in China
Ibn Battuta (Morocco, *c*.1304–1369): Travelled in E Africa, Arabia, China
Bartolomeu Dias (Port., d. 1500): First European to round Cape of Good Hope
Christopher Columbus (Italy, 1451–1506): Made four voyages to Caribbean
Amerigo Vespucci (Italy, 1451–1512): Sailed to Caribbean and S America
Vasco da Gama (Port., *c*.1469–1524): Pioneered eastern sea route to India
John Cabot (Italy, 1461–1498): Sailed across North Atlantic to Canada
Ferdinand Magellan (Port., *c*.1480–1521): Led first expedition round world

Captain Cook with the Maoris of New Zealand

FURTHER FACTS

● When Columbus landed on Hispaniola, about 300,000 Arawaks were living there. By 1548, European diseases, murder by the Spanish and death from work as slaves had reduced the islanders to about 500.
● The continent of America was named after Amerigo Vespucci, an Italian who sailed with the second expedition to visit northern South America in 1499.

37

The East: India, China and Japan

The most popular travel book in medieval Europe was Marco Polo's account of his years of service in the court of the Mongol ruler of China, Kublai Khan. The achievements of the great Asian empires were not mere traveller's tales. Cut off from most outside contact, the Japanese developed a unique civilization of their own. Inventions as diverse as gunpowder and the magnetic compass were used in China centuries before they were known in the West. In India the Moguls ruled a great empire half the size of Europe.

1368–1644	1500s–1700s	1630s
Ming dynasty sees period of Chinese prosperity	Mogul period in India	Japanese close their country to foreigners

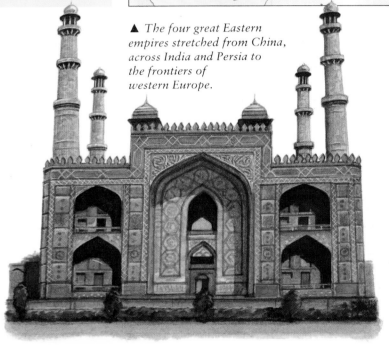

▲ The four great Eastern empires stretched from China, across India and Persia to the frontiers of western Europe.

THE OTTOMAN EMPIRE

For 500 years the Ottoman empire was a great Islamic world power. It was founded in northern Turkey at the end of the 1300s. As devout Muslims, the Ottomans believed it their duty to fight to defend their religion against unbelievers. In a series of jihads (holy wars), they enlarged their empire in all directions. The chief victim of Ottoman aggression was the Christian empire of Byzantium. In 1483 the Ottomans captured Constantinople; it became the capital of their empire until the 1800s. The empire reached its greatest extent under Suleiman the Magnificent. His army overran the Balkans, and only his failure to capture the Austrian capital Vienna in 1529 (below) prevented an invasion of western Europe.

▲ In 1526 the Mogul leader Babar conquered northern India and founded an empire. His grandson was the Mogul emperor Akbar, who is buried in a superb tomb at Fatehpur Sikri.

◄ The Moguls were Muslims but Akbar (seen here in battle) won the loyalty of his Indian subjects, most of whom were Hindus, by allowing them to worship in peace. Akbar was also a generous patron of writers, artists and architects.

▼ The architectural masterpiece of the Ming empire was the capital Peking (Beijing). At its heart lay the 'Forbidden City', forbidden to all except the emperor and his household.

▶ The Ming era of Chinese history, from the mid-1300s to mid-1600s, is renowned for its delicate blue and white porcelain.

Ming vase

Peking
JAPAN
CHINA
MING EMPIRE

CATHOLIC MISSIONARIES

Catholic missionaries arrived in the East in the 1500s. They founded a community in China which lasted until modern times. Japanese Christianity was wiped out in 1638, when 30,000 converts were massacred near Nagasaki.

Seismograph

Chinese cannon

◀ Paper, printing, guns, gunpowder, rockets, compasses, bridges made of cast iron, seed drills, seismographs, steel, umbrellas, paper money – all were invented in China long before they were first used in the West.

Shogun

Samurai warrior

▶ From 1339 to 1573 civil war raged in Japan. In spite of the disorder, the arts flourished. The Golden Pavilion was built (1394) in Kyoto, Japan's capital city from 794 until 1868.

▼ Japanese women practice the Tea Ceremony in the 1700s. Tea-drinking is an ancient Japanese ritual; it shows the formal behaviour of Japanese life.

▲ From the 1100s to the 1800s Japan was ruled by military dictators who bore the title of shogun. The samurai were the warrior class of Japan, whose code of bravery, loyalty and honour was known as bushido.

The Colonization of America

Spaniards began to settle on the Caribbean island of Hispaniola in 1493, a year after Columbus's first landing. In 1496, a few Spanish soldiers slaughtered thousands of rebellious native Arawaks. This pattern of oppression and murder was repeated in Mexico and Peru on a far larger scale by the expeditions of the Spanish conquistadores under Cortés and Pizarro. A century later, the early settlers in New England gradually drove out groups of Native Americans in order to occupy their land.

NORTH AMERICA

AZTEC EMPIRE

• Tenochtitlán
MEXICO

• Quito

PERU
Amazon

SOUTH AMERICA

Lima • • Machu Picchu
Cuzco

INCA EMPIRE

Route of Cortés 1519–1522

Route of Pizarro 1532–1534

Spanish empire in Americas

1492–1504	1541–1542	1733
Columbus's four voyages to America	Orellana first European to cross S America	Foundation of Georgia, the last of the original 13 Colonies

▶ *In 1519, Spanish soldiers led by Cortés landed in Mexico to plunder the fabled wealth of the Aztecs. Pizarro arrived in Peru in 1532 and within two years, he had overthrown the Inca empire. The first North American colonies (opposite page) were settled by immigrants from several European countries.*

◀ *In 1519 the Aztec ruler Montezuma welcomed Hernán Cortés to his capital of Tenochtitlán and showered him with gifts. The early goodwill soon turned to enmity and the Spaniards besieged the city. Aztec wood and stone weapons were no match for steel swords and crossbows. By 1521 the entire Aztec empire had fallen to the Spanish.*

BRAZIL'S ORIGIN

In the 1400s Portuguese navigators travelling to India often sailed far across the Atlantic Ocean to pick up the currents that would sweep them round the Cape of Good Hope. In 1500, on one of these voyages, a fleet led by Pedro Cabral was swept too far west. They reached the coast of Brazil, which they claimed for Portugal.

▶ *In 1532 Spanish conquistadores under Francisco Pizarro kidnapped the Inca emperor Atahualpa. Pizarro's plan was to terrify the Inca army that faced his tiny band of 159 men by capturing their emperor, who was also their god. The plot worked and the Spanish soldiers then killed more than 4000 unarmed Inca nobles. Within hours, Pizarro was master of the Inca capital, Cuzco. Atahualpa was executed in 1533.*

Spanish conquistadores capture Atahualpa

40

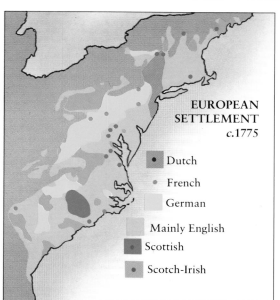

EUROPEAN SETTLEMENT
c.1775

- ● Dutch
- ● French
- ▨ German
- ▨ Mainly English
- ▨ Scottish
- ● Scotch-Irish

HUDSON'S BAY COMPANY

French fur-traders founded the first permanent European settlement in what is now Canada in 1604. In 1670 two French traders received the backing from a group of English noblemen to found a company to exploit the fur trade around the shores of Hudson's Bay. At the trading posts that the company set up Native Americans exchanged goods such as beaver and other animal skins for guns. After the English conquered Canada in 1763, the company gained control of the fur trade in the region.

Puritan settler

▼ *The Pilgrim Fathers, who sailed from England in 1620, founded the first permanent European settlement in what is now the USA at Plymouth, Mass.*

New England farmer

New England settlement

New England woman settler

▲ *Between 1620 and 1700 about 400,000 people of European stock, most of them from England or France, were living in North America. The English settled in far greater numbers because the area they settled in was more suitable for farming. Whole communities came out together from England. They cleared the land for cultivation and for raising farm animals. They soon produced most of the necessities of life and before long became independent of their homeland. A college was founded at Harvard in New England as early as 1636.*

European Society in the 1600s

At the beginning of the 1600s the new-found lands of the Americas were still a novelty to the people of Europe. Only the rich could afford its native vegetables and fruits, which later were to change the diet of much of the world. The gulf between the classes widened. The new-style houses of the wealthy were designed to afford a higher degree of comfort and luxury while the hovels of the poor remained dank, dark and insanitary. In England the one place where all classes mingled were the theatres.

SCIENTIFIC ADVANCES
The 1600s saw a scientific revolution with the invention of the telescope (1608), microscope (1618), thermometer (1641), and barometer (1644). Instruments such as these helped scientists gain an accurate picture of the natural world.

Englishman Isaac Newton's reflecting telescope (1668)

1582
Pope Gregory introduces modern calendar

c.1601
First performance of *Hamlet* by William Shakespeare

1665
Isaac Newton discovers force of gravity

▼ *In medieval England the ownership of land set the nobles apart from the rest of the population. But in the late 1500s rich merchants bought land as a way of becoming 'gentlemen'. The splendour of many of the larger houses built at this time demonstrates the growing wealth of the merchant classes.*

◄ *In most European countries, falconry was a popular sport with both kings and commoners.*

17th-century English manor house

▶ *Early visitors to America brought back many foods new to Europe, including maize, potatoes, tomatoes and French beans. Peaches and apricots were also introduced from Asia.*

▲ *Imported cotton from the new colonies was first woven in Europe in the 1600s.*

▲ *New spices such as mace, cloves, pepper and cinnamon were used to flavour food.*

▲ *The Spanish brought the potato to Europe, a food known in South America for 2000 years.*

▲ *Tobacco was first used in France in the 1560s by Jean Nicot.*

◀ *The Dutch artist Rembrandt painted* The Anatomy Lesson of Dr Tulp *in 1642. Anatomy was then quite a new science. A Belgian doctor, Andreas Vesalius, published the first accurate account of the human body's bones and nervous system in 1543.*

FURTHER FACTS

- In the 1600s the smoking of tobacco was thought to keep away the plague.
- Crops failed regularly in the years 1600–1720. The climate in Europe at that time was unusually severe and the period is known as 'The Little Ice Age'.
- Newspapers were started in the 1600s; among the earliest was the single-page *Antwerp Gazette* in Belgium.

▼ *For centuries peasant families had lived in single-roomed, windowless hovels, which they shared with any animals they might possess.*

▼ *About 90 percent of the population of Europe lived on the land. It was a hard life. Wind and water mills, animals and humans were the only sources of power.*

▲ *The harvest was the most important event of a peasant's year. A poor harvest meant hunger and misery.*

Globe theatre

ELIZABETHAN DRAMA

England was the first country to produce great drama after the Reformation. By 1600 London had five theatres, some of them large enough to hold a thousand spectators. Actors, who a few years earlier had been imprisoned as 'rogues and vagabonds' by the English authorities, were now patronized by Queen Elizabeth and her courtiers. The need for new plays to please the growing audiences was answered by young writers such as Marlowe, Johnson and Middleton. The most popular dramatist of them all was William Shakespeare.

▲ *William Shakespeare (1564–1616) is one of the greatest of English-language dramatists.*

◀ *Many of Shakespeare's plays were performed at the Globe theatre, one of the first public theatres in London.*

Africa and the Slave Trade

Powerful, well-developed civilizations existed in Africa centuries before the Europeans arrived. Slavery was a recognized part of most of these societies and when the first Europeans arrived, slaves were among the goods exchanged in trade. At first, only a few slaves were taken but the number rose to millions when slaves began to be transported across the Atlantic to work on the plantations of the European colonies in America. The loss of so many people was a catastrophe for large regions of Africa.

GREAT ZIMBABWE

The ancient city of Great Zimbabwe lies in the modern country of Zimbabwe to which it gave its name. Prehistoric farmers were the first people to occupy Zimbabwe, but the ruins which remain today date from the middle of the 1300s. At that time the city was the centre of a powerful empire which traded as far afield as China. The present-day ruins of Great Zimbabwe consist of a tower, 9 metres high, surrounded by part of a dry stone wall, 240 metres around and 10 metres high.

Pre-1500s	1500s	1700s
Arabs capture and sell Africans as slaves	Europeans begin shipping slaves to New World	Height of transatlantic slave trade

Charles II guinea coin

▶ *The cities of Ife and Benin were the centres of two West African trading kingdoms dating from the 1200s. Both kingdoms produced superb sculptures in bronze, wood and terracotta.*

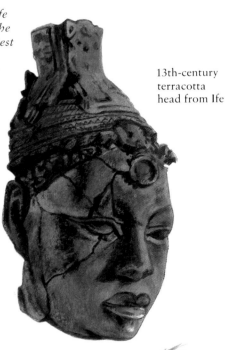

13th-century terracotta head from Ife

FURTHER FACTS

● Denmark first made the slave trade illegal (1792); the US made the trade illegal in 1808. William Wilberforce led the British anti-slavery movement; the trade was abolished in Britain in 1807.
● Desperate slaves sometimes mutined; sailors were known to hold matches near the ships' cannons as a precaution when the slaves were above deck.

▲ *The kingdoms of West Africa were rich in gold. Arabs called the area 'Guinea' and Europeans borrowed the word. In 1663 a coin made of Guinea gold was struck in England by order of Charles II. By the mid-1600s the Guinea coast was supplying most of the New World's slaves.*

▶ *Europeans brought goods such as guns to coastal African rulers to exchange for slaves who had either been kidnapped or were prisoners of war. Many slaves did not survive the voyage to the Americas, often dying from disease, or suicide. After the slaves had been landed, the ships returned to Europe with cargoes of sugar and tobacco.*

► Zanzibar Island lies off the coast of present-day Tanzania on the east coast of Africa. Once Muslims from the Middle East had conquered large parts of North Africa in the AD 600s and 700s, they began to travel south, to trade south of the Sahara Desert. Africans in these regions sold slaves to the Arabs along with ebony and ivory. By the time the Portuguese arrived in Africa in the 1400s the slave trade had been established for hundreds of years.
In 1698 Arabs from the Middle East captured the Portuguese trading post on Zanzibar and made it into a base for slave-trading on the eastern mainland.

▼ In 1482 the Portuguese built a castle at El Mina (now in Ghana) to defend their trade with the gold mines inland. French, Dutch and British merchants soon built their own forts on the west African coast as warehouses for the slave trade.

▼ The Slave Coast was the area between the Gold Coast (now Ghana) and the Niger River. The countries which controlled the slave trade – Britain, France, Holland – had no interest in going further into the interior of the continent. Portugal supplied slaves for Brazil from Angola.

THE GROWTH OF THE SLAVE TRADE, 1526–1810

This painful device prevented the wearer lying down

◄ Newly captured slaves were chained together by the neck or feet and marched in long rows called 'coffles' to the coast to await shipment abroad. Iron collars, sometimes with heavy weights attached, prevented slaves from running away. During the whole Atlantic crossing they were chained in the hold of the ship.

▲ Slave ships were terribly overloaded. Slaves were often packed so tightly that they could only sit or lie flat for the long voyage to the Americas.

Iron manacles

THE AGE OF KINGS

Kings and Commoners

The 1600s was the age of absolute rulers. Not only in Europe, but in India, China and Japan, power was wielded by kings, emperors or shoguns who had total authority over their subjects. Only in England was its king, Charles I, defeated in a civil war and executed by order of parliament. In Europe the most powerful monarchs were Louis XIV of France and Peter the Great of Russia. Peter forced drastic reforms on his backward country.

Louis's reign brought the French monarchy to its zenith, even while his financial extravagance contributed to its destruction less than 70 years after his death. In India, the Moguls built mosques, tombs, citadels and palaces of unparalleled splendour. The 1600s and 1700s also confirmed Europe's world leadership. The growth of their empires overseas was to bring nearly half the world under Europe's control.

▼ *Compared with western Europe, Russia was poor and backward when Peter the Great became tsar in 1682. Peter resolved to make Russia a great power. He toured Europe to recruit technicians and craftsmen. He reformed the government and modernized his army and navy. He also moved his capital to the new city of St Petersburg, which he called his 'window to the West'.*

1643–1715	1649	1682–1725
Reign of Louis XIV of France	Charles I beheaded in England	Reign of Peter the Great of Russia

Peter the Great in England

A jewelled cup given by Peter the Great to his son Alexis

Russian boyars

▲ *The boyars were a group of families who had been the ruling class in Russia since the Middle Ages. Peter abolished their powers and ordered that their beards be cut off as a symbol of their lost authority.*

FURTHER FACTS

● Louis XIV's absolute control of France is epitomized by his supposed remark 'L'état, c'est moi' ('I am the state').
● After Charles I's execution, England became a commonwealth ruled by parliament. In 1653 Oliver Cromwell, a general in the civil war, became lord protector. The monarchy was restored in 1660 when Charles II returned to England.
● A brilliant general, Cromwell was also ruthless, as shown by his forced settlement of Protestants in Catholic Ireland after Ireland rebelled against English rule in 1649.

◄ *Under Peter, Russian labourers (serfs) continued to live in great poverty; in the countryside, people often starved in the harsh Russian winters.*

◀ Like his father James I, Charles I of England believed he had been appointed by God to rule his country. He refused to accept parliamentary control of his policies and imposed taxes without parliament's consent. For 11 years he governed on his own. In 1642 the quarrel between king and parliament developed into a civil war. Charles was supported by the nobles, Anglicans and Catholics. The parliamentary army was mostly made up of working men. After a series of victories by the parliamentarian general Oliver Cromwell, Charles surrendered in 1645. He was put on trial, found guilty of treason and executed in 1649.

▼ Louis XIV built the most magnificent palace in Europe for himself and his court at Versailles, near Paris. No cost was spared, and the finest artists were hired to decorate it with sculptures, carvings and paintings. It was surrounded by beautiful formal gardens. Versailles is considered to be the greatest architectural achievement of the 1600s.

Known as the 'Sun King', Louis XIV's emblem was a golden sun

◀ A tapestry of a scene at the world-famous Gobelins workshops. Louis XIV inspects furnishings intended for Versailles. Louis and his minister Colbert encouraged the establishment of French factories to provide tapestries and other luxurious items for his palaces.

LOUIS XIV'S EXTRAVAGANCE
Louis XIV doubled taxes to raise money for both the building of his palace at Versailles and to keep France in a series of European wars. But the wars brought France no gains and Louis's extravagance created an enormous strain on the country's resources. Six out of every 10 francs collected in taxes had to pay for the building and upkeep of Versailles alone.

The Age of Reason

The Age of Reason, or Enlightenment, was a period from about 1650 to 1750 when people in western Europe believed that everything in nature could be explained by scientific enquiry and reason. This led to a questioning of established beliefs and to support for religious tolerance in much of Europe and the British North American colonies (later the United States). Even despotic rulers such as Frederick the Great of Prussia tried to put the new social and political ideas into practice in their states.

1596–1650
Life of René Descartes. The Age of Reason grew from his ideas

1740
Prussia given freedom of press and worship by Frederick the Great

1751–1776
Denis Diderot publishes his multi-volume *Encyclopédie*

▼ *In 1735 a Swedish doctor, Carl von Linné (known as Linnaeus), produced the first logical system for naming and classifying plants and animals. He gave everything two names. The first part of the name is the* genus *(group), the second part the* species *(kind). In 1801, the French naturalist Jean-Baptiste Lamarck devised a system for classifying animals without backbones (invertebrates).*

◄ *The baroque was the name given to the style of European art in the 1600s. Its leading artist was Rubens, whose paintings for the French court included* The Marriage of Marie de Médicis to Henri IV. *In the 1700s a renewed interest in classical art caused many public buildings in Europe to be modelled on Greek temples (below).*

Old Museum, Berlin, Germany

BALLET AND OPERA
Ballet was developed as an entertainment in the French court of the 1600s. The first public performance was in France in about 1708. The first operas were composed in Italy in the 1590s, but the art form reached greater heights in the works of Gluck and Mozart in the 1700s. Elaborate sets and costumes dazzled the audiences with spectacular effects.

Early ballet dancer

17th-century opera

► *Frederick II of Prussia, known as 'the Great', was perhaps the outstanding monarch of the Age of Reason. Frederick was a brilliant general in war and an able administrator in times of peace. He was a keen student of literature, philosophy and music and played the flute almost as a professional. A talented composer himself, he was a generous patron of other composers, notably of Johann Sebastian Bach. He also corresponded with Voltaire and other leading thinkers of the time.*

▼ *In 1675, Charles II of England founded the Royal Observatory at Greenwich, near London. Its purpose was to provide aids to accurate navigation for ships on the high seas. The Greenwich system of geographical longitude and time-keeping has since become standard throughout the world.*

Frederick the Great playing the flute

FURTHER FACTS

● Frenchman René Descartes, usually called the father of modern philosophy, was also a brilliant mathematician and scientist. Queen Kristina of Sweden hired him to give her lessons in philosophy.
● Denis Diderot's *Encyclopédie* not only condemned the monarchy in France, it also denounced the power of the Catholic Church. The French authorities banned its sale and Diderot was in constant danger of imprisonment.
● The *English Dictionary* (1747–1755), compiled by Dr Samuel Johnson, is the model for all the English-language dictionaries that have appeared since.

▼ *The great work that promoted the humanistic philosophy of the Age of Reason was the* Encyclopédie (1747–1772), *edited by a universal genius, the French philosopher Denis Diderot. The 35 volumes reviewed the arts and sciences of the time.*

JAPANESE ISOLATION
During the 1630s Japan's rulers decided that contact with the West must end. In particular, they feared that Christian missionaries might bring European armies to invade Japan. They therefore banned most foreigners from entering Japan and the Japanese from leaving their country. As a result, people in the West were unable to appreciate the great beauty of the Japanese art of this period until the late 1800s.

Japanese porcelain figures *c.* 1700

European Settlement Overseas

By the beginning of the 1600s, the heyday of Portuguese and Spanish expansion had passed. It was now the French, Dutch and British who built empires overseas. Most of their colonies were not established by governments but by groups of merchants organized into trading companies, such as the Dutch and British East India Companies. The company was granted the right to trade in the area by the local ruler. Later the trading companies were dissolved and their possessions became part of their country's empire.

1600	1641	1763
British East India Company founded	Dutch seize Malacca from Portuguese	Peace of Paris ends Seven Years' War

▲ *The first Europeans to settle along the Hudson River Valley, in present-day New York state, were the Dutch. In 1625 they built a trading post on Manhattan Island which they had bought from the Native Americans. The British captured the colony in 1664 and renamed it New York.*

▶ *The Dutch East India Company was set up in 1602 to promote and defend Dutch trade with the East Indies. By 1641 the company had taken the place of the Portuguese as controllers of the valuable East Indian spice trade. In 1652 the company founded a base at the Cape of Good Hope as a staging post for Dutch ships on the voyage from Europe to the East Indies. This began Dutch settlement in South Africa.*

▲ *Samuel de Champlain (c.1570–1635) was one of the founders of the French colonies in North America. In 1603 he explored the St Lawrence River in Canada. In 1608 he built a fur-trading post on its shores which he called Quebec.*

▶ *The Seven Years' War (1756–1763) involved several European powers; France and Britain were in conflict because of a longtime rivalry for colonial supremacy in India and North America. The fate of the North American colonies was decided in 1759 when a British force led by General James Wolfe captured Quebec, the capital of New France (present-day Canada). Quebec's fall ensured that Britain gained all of France's lands in North America.*

EUROPEAN EMPIRES, c.1770

- Spanish
- Portuguese
- British
- Dutch
- French
- Russian (c.1763)

CANADA

RUSSIAN EMPIRE

Great Britain

Netherlands

France

Portugal — Spain

OTTOMAN EMPIRE

MANCHU CHINA

LOUISIANA

THIRTEEN COLONIES

NEW SPAIN

INDIA

PHILIPPINES

NEW GRANADA

AFRICA

PERU   BRAZIL

INDONESIA

RIO DE LA PLATA

NEW HOLLAND

Musketeers aboard the British warship *Centurion*, 1752

▲ *Spain and Portugal were the first European countries to build empires overseas. The Portuguese focused their efforts on Africa and Asia. The Spanish occupied all of South America except for Brazil. The English and French settled in North America. Dutch traders colonized the East Indies.*

▶ *During the 1700s European colonial powers were frequently at war with each other. Since the colonies could only be reached by ship, many clashes took place at sea. A major objective in war was to interfere with the enemy's trade and to seize enemy ships. Here, British musketeers on the warship* Centurion *fire on the* Covadonga, *loaded with silver from the Spanish colony of Mexico.*

FURTHER FACTS

- In the 1600s and 1700s the term 'East Indies' was originally used to describe India; later it came to refer to southeast Asia, especially Indonesia.
- The only country in Asia never to be colonized by any European power was Siam (now Thailand).
- In 1756 a number of British prisoners were shut up in a small room during a battle between British and Indian troops. Several died in the suffocating heat. The British greatly exaggerated the size of the room and the number of deaths. The incident became known among the British as 'The Black Hole of Calcutta'.

Tipu's tiger

◀ *In 1757 British East India Company troops defeated the ruler of Bengal at Plassey, northern India. With French influence in decline, the victory made Britain the dominant power in India. However, Indian rulers such as Tipu, ruler of Mysore, continued to defy the British. Tipu ('tiger') had a model made showing a tiger eating a British soldier.*

THE AGE OF REVOLUTIONS

The American War of Independence

The colonists of the Thirteen Colonies of British North America were governed from London. They were treated as British subjects except that they did not have the vote and therefore nobody to represent their interests in parliament. When parliament passed laws which imposed new taxes, the colonies rebelled. In the revolution that followed the colonists won their independence from Britain and set up a republic. The success of the Americans in overthrowing a ruling authority was an inspiration to the peoples of Europe who lived under repressive regimes. Within a few years of the American's revolution, the French had risen against their king and ruling classes. After several years of violence and bloodshed they established a republic which in its turn became the model for revolutionaries throughout the world.

1775–1776
Early fighting around Boston

Sept. 1777
Americans win key battle of Saratoga

Sept. 1783
Britain recognizes independence of the United States

◀ *The 'Boston Tea Party' was a protest against taxation in Britain's North American colonies. The colonists objected to paying taxes on items such as tea, imposed by the British parliament without their consent. A small band of colonists dressed up as Mohawk Indians, boarded three ships in Boston harbour and dumped tea chests in the sea. The British reacted with a series of punitive laws known as the 'Intolerable Acts', which included the closure of the port of Boston until money was paid to the East India Company for the loss of the tea.*

▶ *The Declaration of Independence, adopted on 4 July 1776, is the foundation document of the United States of America. It proclaimed the separation of the American colonies (which now became states) from Britain. A lawyer, Thomas Jefferson (centre), was the principal author. The document was signed by 56 delegates of the Thirteen Colonies. Since 1776, 4 July has been a national holiday in the USA.*

The Liberty Bell in Philadelphia is a symbol of American independence

Draft of the Declaration of Independence

Quebec
Montreal
Saratoga
Great Lakes
Lexington/ Concord
Bunker Hill
Princeton
Extent of American Colonies
Yorktown
INDIAN TERRITORY
Camden
FLORIDA

▲ George Washington became commander of the American forces in 1775. On Christmas night 1776, Washington crossed the Delaware river, before beating the British in the battles of Trenton and Princeton. Washington's greatest achievement was to keep 16,000 volunteer troops together during five years of conflict in which they suffered many reverses.

▲ Early in the war the British captured New York (1776). The war ended with their surrender at Yorktown (1781). A turning point was the American alliance with the French in 1778.

▼ The British victory at Bunker Hill (1775) cost them 1000 casualties against 400 American casualties. Their well-drilled troops trained for European wars stood in close-packed ranks firing volleys of shot in the direction of the enemy. The Americans, used to killing game and fighting on the frontiers with Native Americans, were skilled marksmen who could put a bullet through a man's head at 200 paces.

American revolutionary soldier

British grenadier c. 1775

KEY DATES

● **April 1775:** The first shots of the war were fired at Lexington near Boston, when British troops arrived to destroy the arms store of the local militia.

● **June 1775:** George Washington becomes commander of the rebel American army.

● **March 1776:** The British evacuate Boston.

● **4 July 1776:** The Declaration of Independence is adopted by delegates of the 13 Colonies.

● **October 1781:** The British are besieged at Yorktown by the Americans and their French allies.

● **September 1783:** US and Britain sign final peace treaty in Paris.

The French Revolution

The revolution in France of 1789 is one of the most important events in human history. It is important because it overthrew a powerful monarchy and introduced new principles of democratic government. The revolution was extremely violent, killing both the French king and thousands of citizens. France was in chaos as one group of revolutionaries after another failed to establish firm government. Eventually, the French army seized power, led by its most successful general, Napoleon Bonaparte.

July 1789
Mobs storm the Bastille; the revolution begins

July 1794
Robespierre executed; the Terror ends

November 1799
Napoleon overthrows the revolutionary government

▲ *Louis XVI was shy and stupid rather than bad or cruel. He preferred hunting to governing his country. He was also unfortunate in having an unpopular wife, the pleasure-loving Marie Antoinette. In 1793 he was to pay with his life for his indifference to the misery that heavy taxation was causing ordinary French people.*

▲ *By 1789 the States-General (a national parliament) had not met since 1614. In June the Third Estate (the commoners in the parliament) met in a tennis court where they took an oath not to disband until France had a new assembly and constitution. The Tennis Court Oath was the beginning of the revolution.*

▶ *Although Louis XVI gave in to the Third Estate and ordered that a new National Assembly should meet, rumours spread through Paris that the king would soon disband it. The rumours started riots both outside Paris and in the city itself, where on 14 July an angry mob captured the Bastille prison, a symbol to Parisians of royal power.*

◀ In 1789 many working men and women in Paris were jobless and hungry. On 14 July the price of bread was doubled. The unemployed joined shopkeepers and tradesmen to form the mob that stormed the Bastille.

Woman revolutionary with tricolor rosette in her hat

Revolutionaries were called *sans culottes* because they wore trousers rather than breeches (unlike the nobility)

KEY DATES

● **1789:** France was divided by law into three groups called Estates. The First Estate was the clergy; the Second Estate, the nobility; the Third Estate, the commons (town corporations).
● **June 1789:** The Tennis Court Oath.
● **June 1791:** The royal family is caught trying to leave France and brought back to Paris.
● **January 1793:** The king, Louis XVI, executed. His queen, Marie Antoinette, was guillotined in October 1793.
● **September 1793–July 1794:** Reign of Terror; ends with death of Robespierre.
● **1795–1799:** France ruled by a five-member Directory.

UNITÉ
INDIVISIBILITÉ
DE LA
RÉPUBLIQUE
LIBERTÉ
ÉGALITÉ
FRATERNITÉ
OU LA
MORT

▶ Slogans such as 'unity, liberty, equality and fraternity or death' were seen on the revolutionary posters stuck up in Paris.

◀ The period from mid 1793 to mid 1794 is called the Terror. France was then ruled by the Jacobins, a group of extremist revolutionaries led by Maximilian Robespierre. The Jacobins ruled by fear. Thousands of innocent people from all classes were condemned for their opposition to the revolution. Large crowds watched the public executions on the guillotine.

Napoleon Bonaparte

Napoleon Bonaparte seized power in France when the government turned to the army for support. Napoleon was the army's most successful general. From 1799 Napoleon led a number of brilliant military campaigns that won him control of most of western Europe. His one major defeat was at Trafalgar in 1805, which gave Britain command of the seas. From 1812 Napoleon's fortunes declined. His armies retreated from Russia and he lost a series of battles in Germany. His defeat at Waterloo in 1815 ended his career.

▼ *In 1799 Napoleon made himself first consul (a form of dictator). To confirm his position he took the title of Emperor of France in 1804. At his coronation Napoleon took the crown from the pope and placed it on his own head as a sign of his personal power. He followed this by crowning his wife, Josephine as empress. The first French republic was now ended.*

1799	1812	1815
Napoleon becomes first consul of France	French army retreats from Russia	Napoleon finally beaten at battle of Waterloo

▶ *The only force that continually foiled Napoleon's ambitions was the British navy. Under Horatio Nelson, the British won a number of key sea battles such as Trafalgar (1805), when Nelson was killed. At the time of the Napoleonic Wars, life on board naval ships was extremely harsh. Up to 24 lashes with a whip was the usual punishment for the often mutinous sailors. Even this painful ordeal was imposed by some captains as an act of mercy. The alternative was a court martial which might sentence a man to hundreds of lashes, or to death.*

▲ One of Napoleon's most famous battles was at Eylau, now in Poland (1807), when in a snowstorm his army withstood heavy losses to hold off a far larger Russian army.

▲ By 1810 Napoleon controlled most of Europe, including several German states and much of Poland. He made members of his family the rulers of Spain, Italy and the Netherlands.

FURTHER FACTS

● By destroying the joint Franco-Spanish fleet at Trafalgar in 1805, the British navy saved Britain from invasion.
● In 1814 Napoleon was defeated by the armies of a European coalition at Leipzig. He abdicated and was exiled on the island of Elba. In March 1815 he escaped from Elba and raised a new army. He was finally defeated by the British and Prussians at the battle of Waterloo in June 1815.

▲ In 1812 Napoleon made the disastrous decision to invade Russia; the Russians were his only remaining rivals on mainland Europe. His army reached Moscow in September 1812 to find that the Russians had burned it down. The French army was not equipped to survive the harsh Russian winter which was just beginning. Napoleon ordered a withdrawal. As the French retreated, three quarters of the 500,000-strong army was killed by the Russians, or died of cold and hunger.

▲ After his final defeat at Waterloo, Napoleon gave himself up to the British to escape being executed by the Prussians. The British sent him to the remote Atlantic island of St Helena, where he died in 1821.

THE AGE OF IMPERIALISM

The Industrial Revolution

The Industrial Revolution is a term describing major changes in the economic and social structure of many western countries in the 1700s and 1800s. At the beginning of the 1700s most of Europe's people lived and worked on the land. By the time the 1800s ended, most Europeans were city dwellers, earning a living in factories or offices. As work became unavailable on the land huge numbers of Europeans migrated overseas, particularly to America. The political map of Europe was also redrawn during this period. Revolutions convulsed the continent from the 1820s to the 1870s. They swept away states ruled by hereditary families and replaced them with new nations based on shared history, culture and language. The European powers also strove to win new colonial territories in Africa and to extend their empires in Asia and the Pacific.

1787	1789–1815	1833
In US John Fitch demonstrates first workable steamboat	France's industrial revolution stopped by revolution and wars	British Factory Act bans children under nine working in factories

THE FIRST INDUSTRIAL REVOLUTION

Britain's industrial revolution was the period (1750–1850) when Britain's dominance of overseas markets through its empire, and the availability at home of coal and iron ore, transformed it from a farming to a manufacturing community. The harnessing of steam power and major new inventions led to cheap mass-manufacture of materials such as cotton. Iron, made by the new processes, was strong enough for building structures like bridges in a different way.

The world's first iron bridge, built in England, 1777

▶ *The transitions of Britain's industrial revolution were repeated elsewhere as other western countries became industrialized. Farmworkers moved to the towns, seeking work in the new factories. The densely-packed, low-quality houses built for them soon became unhealthy slums.*

New factory

Workers' housing

Eli Whitney's cotton gin

Canal

Canal barge

▶ *In Britain a system of canals linking the major rivers was built, providing the cheap transport the new factories needed to deliver raw materials and take away finished goods. The goods were loaded onto barges pulled by horses along tracks called towpaths. Canal-building reached its peak in Britain in the 1790s. Later in the Industrial Revolution, goods could be moved more easily on the newly-built railways.*

◄ *Before the new machines led to manufacture in factories, cloth was made in homes. Women and children did the spinning. Weaving was traditionally men's work.*

▼ *George Stephenson opened the first public railway in 1825, between Stockton and Darlington in Yorkshire. In 1835 his son Robert built the engine for the first German train, Der Adler (The Eagle).*

Early German train (1835)

► *In the early 1800s, children as young as five years old worked underground in the mines. They often had to work shifts of 12 hours and more. Some toiled half-naked, chained to carts laden with coal which they pulled along dark passageways. Factories also used children. The usual shift was 15 hours a day. Many children were orphans; they lived in crowded, dirty hostels where the death rate could reach 60 percent.*

▼ *In the 1700s a revolution also took place in British farming. Jethro Tull's seed drill and improved ploughs raised the standard of cultivation. Animals that in an earlier age would have been slaughtered in the winter were now kept alive on root crops. Between 1700 and 1800, the yield of wheat doubled. Selective breeding meant larger, healthier livestock.*

Jethro Tull's seed drill

Improved cattle and sheep

FURTHER FACTS

● Hargreaves introduced his 8-thread spinning machine, (called 'jenny' after his wife) in 1764. A later model was able to spin 120 threads.
● After Britain, the next western country to become industrialized was Belgium.
● By the 1840s France, Germany, Belgium and the US had all begun to build railways; the coming of the railways revolutionized travel as ordinary people were able to move about more easily.
● Towns grew rapidly: in Britain, in 1801 Manchester's population was 75,000. By 1851 it was 303,000.

The New Nationalism

Napoleon's domination of Europe at the beginning of the 1800s created a renewed desire for liberty and the pride in nationality which had inspired the French Revolution. Greece and Belgium were the first to throw off the old order and gain independence. In South America, after twenty years of uprisings and wars, independent states replaced the old empires of Spain and Portugal. By the 1870s, both Italy and Germany had become unified, and Germany had become a major new world power.

1821–1827 War of Greek Independence	**1848** Year of revolutions in Europe	**1871** Germany united under Prussian leadership

▶ *The Ottoman Turks had conquered Greece in the 1500s but the Greeks never forgot they were a nation. In 1821 they rebelled against Turkish rule. In 1827 Russia, Britain and France agreed to use force if necessary to help the Greeks gain their independence. When Turkey refused to give up control of Greece, a joint French, Russian and British force defeated the Turkish fleet in Navarino Bay. The battle helped Greece become independent in 1832.*

19th-century Greek soldier

Battle of Navarino

Garibaldi embarks for Sicily

◀ *Giuseppe Garibaldi was the hero of the Italian Risorgimento – the movement to replace Austrian and French rule with unification and independence. In May 1860 he landed in Sicily with a thousand red-shirted followers. In August he crossed to the mainland and captured Naples. Garibaldi's example inspired his fellow patriots to continue the struggle which was finally won when Rome became the capital of a united Italy in 1870.*

◄ In Europe, 1848 was a year of revolutions. There were revolts in Germany, Italy, Poland and Hungary. The rulers of France and Austria gave up their thrones after major uprisings.

▼ In July 1870 France went to war with Prussia, the leading state of Germany. The war was a disaster for France. Its armies were destroyed and Paris came under siege. The city's defenders held out for four months but in January 1871 they were forced by starvation to surrender. The victory united the German states. In 1871 King Wilhelm of Prussia became emperor of all Germany.

The Arc de Triomphe is protected as Parisians leave before the 1870 siege

KARL MARX

The ideas of the German philosopher Karl Marx inspired the worldwide communist movements of the 1900s. He wanted all political power to belong to the working class. Most of his writing and research was done in London, where he lived in exile from 1849. His most important works were the *Communist Manifesto* (published in Paris during the 1848 Revolution) and *Das Kapital*.

Simón Bolívar

INDEPENDENCE IN SOUTH AMERICA

The peoples of the Spanish South American empire were inspired by the French Revolution to fight for their freedom. Mexico won independence in 1821. Simón Bolívar's armies fought for the independence of Colombia and Bolivia. José San Martín liberated Chile and, with Bolívar, freed Colombia and Ecuador.

MEXICO 1821
CENTRAL AMERICAN FEDERATION 1821–1838
VENEZUELA 1830
British
Dutch
French colonies in Guyana
COLOMBIA 1819
ECUADOR 1830
BRAZIL 1822
PERU 1821
BOLIVIA 1825
PARAGUAY 1811
CHILE 1818
URUGUAY 1828
ARGENTINA 1810

FURTHER FACTS

● In 1830 the French deposed their king, Charles X. Louis Philippe became king until the 1848 revolution.

● The 1830 French uprising encouraged the Belgians to rebel against their Dutch rulers. Belgium became independent in 1833.

● In 1830 and 1863 Polish patriots rebelled against Russian rule. Both uprisings failed and many Poles were exiled to Siberia.

The American Civil War

In 1861 seven (later eleven) southern states of the USA declared themselves a separate nation, the Confederate States of America. The northern (Union) states then went to war with the South to preserve the country's unity. The cause of the row between the two regions was slavery. The agricultural South wished to retain it; the industrial North was determined to end it. The South lost the civil war as, despite early military success, it was overwhelmed by the superior forces and industrial might of the North.

1860
Abraham Lincoln elected United States' president

1865
The Union wins the American Civil War

1869
First American transcontinental railway completed

▲ The Confederates rejected the Stars and Stripes and adopted their own flags. Their troops wore grey uniforms. The Union troops wore blue.

Abraham Lincoln in 1861

Slaves picking cotton

◄ The economy of the southern states was based on black slave labour. The new president, Abraham Lincoln, and his Republican party wanted to limit slavery. Afraid of being outvoted by northern non-slave states, the southern states under Jefferson Davis left the Union. War broke out in April 1861.

▼ New, more effective, long-range guns made the American Civil War one of the bloodiest wars in history. Three million men fought in it and over 600,000 died. However, twice as many died from disease as were killed in action.

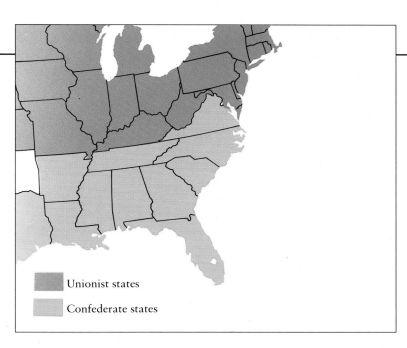

▶ *The division of the United States at the beginning of the American Civil War. Eleven of the 34 US states made up the Confederacy. The civil war took place over a vast area. For the first time in history, railways played a vital part in warfare by moving troops and supplies swiftly over great distances.*

▊ Unionist states

▊ Confederate states

FURTHER FACTS

● America's first railroad opened in South Carolina in 1830.
● The civil war began in April 1861, when Confederate artillery fired on Union troops at Fort Sumter. It ended in April 1865 when the Confederates surrendered at Appomattox, Virginia.
● A major turning point of the civil war was the Union victory at Gettysburg, Pennsylvania in July 1863; the South then abandoned its hopes of invading the Union.
● In 1869 the first railway to cross the US cut in two the buffalo herds on which the Plains tribes depended for food and clothing. By 1900 the tribes had all been moved to reservations.

WINNING THE WEST

In 1803, the United States bought France's claim to the lands west of the Mississippi river for $15 million and so doubled the new country's size. The purchase of this new land began a movement to the western territories of thousands of people, seeking their fortunes and a better life. The move west increased after the civil war in the 1860s. But the land was not empty. Native American tribes had lived on the Plains for many generations. The new settlers found they could only build and farm there if they first drove the local tribes away.

Wagon train, travelling to American West

SETTLER TRAILS ACROSS THE USA

CANADA

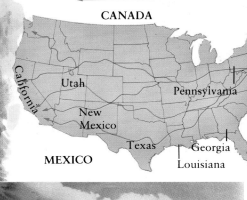

California
Utah
Pennsylvania
New Mexico
Texas
Georgia
Louisiana

MEXICO

▶ *The first American railroad was opened in 1830. By 1880, America's rail network exceeded that of Europe. Rail transport overcame the great distances which had hindered the development of America. It made sending goods to markets cheap and easy. In return it brought back the factory-made equipment that the Midwestern farmers needed.*

The Movement of Peoples

European migration to America gathered pace after the American War of Independence. During the 1800s, millions more crossed the Atlantic. Driven out by famine, the numbers of Irish emigrants overtook those from the rest of Britain. More emigrants came from Germany, Sweden and later Italy, Russia and eastern Europe. In its early years Australia had been a British prison colony. The discovery of gold in the mid-1800s increased the flow of people to both Australia and North America.

USA 33.6 m 1821–1920
S America 3.6 m
Australia and New Zealand 2 m

Arrows show numbers in millions

▲ Most of the Europeans who emigrated during the 1800s went to the United States. Other favoured destinations were Australia and New Zealand and the countries of South America.

1815–1914	1840s	1867
Main period of European migration	Potato famine begins in Ireland	Britain ends transportation to Australia

Sydney Harbour in the early 1800s

A CONVICT SETTLEMENT

In the 1700s convicted criminals in Britain were sometimes sentenced to hard labour in its colonies overseas. Most went to North America. After the US won independence in 1776, Britain established a new penal colony at Botany Bay in Australia. Convicts were shipped to parts of Australia until the 1860s.

▲ New South Wales in eastern Australia was founded as a British prison colony. A group of convicts and guards arrived on the site of the future city of Sydney in 1788. Before then the people who lived there were Aborigines. From the 1820s free settlers were allowed to immigrate. The rearing of sheep in the rich pastures near the coasts created a profitable wool industry. By 1900 Sydney had a population of 400,000.

FURTHER FACTS

- A penal colony was established on the island of Tasmania off the coast of mainland Australia in 1803; 65,000 convicts served their sentences there.
- By the 1870s every one of the Australian Aborigines who had lived on the island of Tasmania was dead. Some had perished from European diseases; white settlers had murdered the rest.
- European immigration into the US was at its height during 1901–1910, with 8,795,386 people admitted. Of those, over 6 million came from southern and eastern Europe.

Prospector panning for gold

◀ In 1848 gold was discovered in California. Within a few months a gold rush had started. The nearest port, San Francisco, grew from a small town to a city of 25,000 as prospectors and other people massed to seek their fortune. In the late 1800s there were also gold rushes in Canada, South Africa, New Zealand and Australia.

▶ Dawson, northeastern Canada, was typical of the towns that sprang up almost overnight in the newly discovered gold fields. At the height of the gold rush in the Yukon in the 1890s Dawson had about 25,000 residents.

THE IRISH POTATO FAMINE
The main food of the Irish people was the potato. Between 1845–1851 the crop failed. About a million people died of hunger and another million people emigrated, mostly to the US. Millions more have emigrated since. Today Ireland's population is about half the 8 million it was before 1845.

▼ Immigration into America between 1815 and 1914 was the largest peaceful movement of people in history. It is estimated that about 35 million people entered the US during that time. Thousands of Chinese landed in the west coast states until the US Congress restricted further entry in 1882. The overwhelming majority of the immigrants came from Europe. From 1892–1924 the chief entry point to the US was Ellis Island in New York Bay. Here, would-be immigrants (below) were interviewed by immigration officers.

Society in the 1800s

The taste and the standards of the prosperous middle class set the pattern of the West in the Victorian Age (named after Queen Victoria, who ruled from 1837 to 1901). They were highminded, for their education was dominated by Christian teaching; their life centred on the family and the home. A great many men and women were employed as domestic servants in the homes of the middle and upper classes. They received free food and lodging and a small wage but in return they worked up to 70 hours a week.

1837–1901
The 63-year reign of Queen Victoria

1860s
Victorian style in design reaches its peak

1890s
Reaction against Victorian style

▲ Most of the servants of middle-class families lived on the premises in simply-furnished rooms in the attic or cellar.

Middle-class Victorians

▼ The upper middle classes in Victorian times enjoyed a highly privileged life-style. They lived in imposing villas set in large grounds in leafy suburbs. They did no housework. A staff of servants ranging from the lordly butler down to the lowly scullery maid attended to all their needs.

Brass four poster bed

Butler serves tea in drawing room

19th-century house, Boston, US

Kitchen

◄ Servants rose at six in summer and winter. In winter, grates had to be cleaned and blacked, and fresh fires lit. After the room had been dusted the family's breakfast was laid. Later, the mistress of the house might discuss with her cook what food needed to be bought for the day's main meals.

VISITING THE POOR
Many well-off people had a sense of duty towards those less fortunate than themselves. They supported societies to reform prisons and to prevent cruelty to children. They gave food and clothing to the sick and needy, and visited them in their homes.

LOUIS PASTEUR
By the 1800s the work of scientists had improved the health of people in the West. The French scientist Louis Pasteur introduced a process which kills harmful organisms in foods. He also developed the first vaccines against anthrax and rabies.

Benz three-wheeled car

Early 'boneshaker' bicycle

▼ An army of street vendors peopled city streets in the 1800s. Among them were sellers of flowers, cottons, saucepans, cage-birds, songs and fake medicines. Food and drink was also sold – chestnuts, hot pies, ice cream, vegetables and spices. The streets were also full of workers such as sweeps on their way to jobs.

Chimney sweep

Flowergirl

Early electric light bulb

Bell's first telephone

Pie man

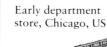

▲ The 1800s was an age of invention. From America came telephones, the carpet sweeper, cash registers, the safety pin, condensed milk, fruit machines and barbed wire. British inventors contributed the electric lamp, the pneumatic tyre, shorthand and linoleum. The Germans, Daimler and Benz, developed the motor car. The first successful bicycle appeared in France.

Early department store, Chicago, US

DEPARTMENT STORES
Before the mid-1800s shops usually specialized in the goods they sold. The first department store (a shop stocking a wide variety of goods) opened in New York in 1848. Others soon opened across America and in western Europe.

The Colonial Age

The Industrial Revolution caused the new industrial powers to seach for raw materials for their factories, mineral wealth such as gold for investment and new markets for their goods. European powers began to acquire many new colonies, especially in Africa, southeast Asia and the islands of the Pacific Ocean. From the 1870s to 1910, in the 'Scramble for Africa', almost the whole of that continent was colonized by Europeans who needed its abundant supply of raw materials.

1817–1818
The British dominance of India begins

1860
French begin expansion in West Africa

1898
Spain cedes Philippines to the US

Commodore Perry in Japan, 1853

▶ *In 1857 a mutiny by sepoys, the Indian soldiers in the British army in India, grew into a widespread revolt against British rule. The mutineers seized Lucknow and India's capital, Delhi. Cawnpore was captured and its British residents murdered. The British called up reinforcements and retook the captured cities, including Delhi (right). By July 1858 the rebels were defeated and the British were again in control of India.*

▲ *Japan had been isolated by its rulers from foreign contact, from the 1600s until the mid-1800s. The western powers tried, unsuccessfully, to gain admittance. In 1853 American warships under Commodore Matthew Perry anchored in Tokyo Bay. The threat of American naval power helped Perry persuade the Japanese to resume trading with the West.*

EUROPEAN COLONIES IN THE 1800s

As the 1800s ended, Britain, France and the Netherlands occupied most of south and southeast Asia. The British ruled India, Burma and Malaya. France had absorbed Vietnam. The United States had taken the Philippines from Spain in the war of 1898. The Dutch had ruled most of the East Indies ever since driving out the Portuguese in the early 1600s, but Germany occupied part of New Guinea and Britain controlled Brunei, Sarawak and North Borneo. Of all the south Asian countries, only the kingdom of Siam was not under foreign rule. By 1914 the whole of Africa with the exception of Ethiopia and Liberia, had either been colonized or was supervised by a European power *(see opposite page)*. Territory controlled by Britain stretched almost unbroken from Egypt to South Africa. France possessed most of West and North Africa. Germany, Italy, Portugal and Spain held the rest of the continent.

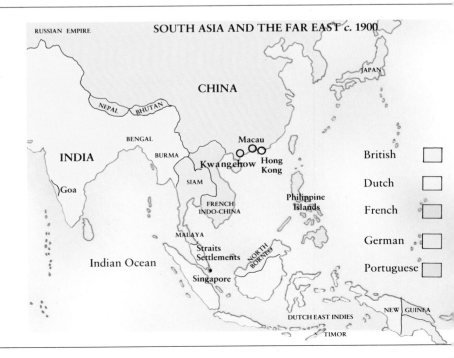

SOUTH ASIA AND THE FAR EAST c. 1900

RUSSIAN EMPIRE
JAPAN
CHINA
NEPAL BHUTAN
BENGAL
INDIA
BURMA
Macau
Kwangchow Hong Kong
SIAM
Goa
FRENCH INDO-CHINA
Philippine Islands
MALAYA
Straits Settlements
NORTH BORNEO
Indian Ocean
Singapore
NEW GUINEA
DUTCH EAST INDIES
TIMOR

British
Dutch
French
German
Portuguese

▼ *In the scramble for colonies, France claimed rights over Vietnam in SE Asia. French Catholic missionaries had been in Vietnam since the 1600s.*

After defeating the Vietnamese in a long series of wars the French made Vietnam a colony in 1887 (as French Indochina).

French soldiers fighting in North Vietnam, 1853

► *In 1839 the Chinese tried to stop the illegal importing of opium by the British. When they destroyed a large cargo of the drug, the British retaliated by landing troops and taking the city of Shanghai. Fighting only ended in 1856 with the seizure of Peking by an Anglo-French force; this opened Chinese ports to western trade.*

▼ *Throughout the 1800s European explorers and Christian missionaries travelled deep into Africa. In 1866 the Scottish missionary and explorer, David Livingstone, disappeared while seeking the sources of Nile. In a famous meeting, the American journalist H.M. Stanley met him by Lake Tanganyika.*

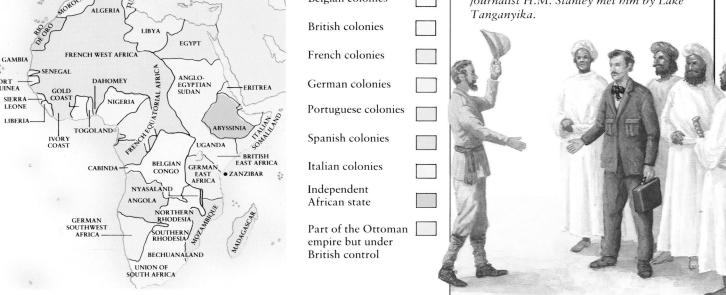

AFRICA IN 1914

Belgian colonies ☐

British colonies ☐

French colonies ☐

German colonies ☐

Portuguese colonies ☐

Spanish colonies ☐

Italian colonies ☐

Independent African state ☐

Part of the Ottoman empire but under British control ☐

MOROCCO
RIO DE ORO
ALGERIA
TUNISIA
LIBYA
EGYPT
GAMBIA
FRENCH WEST AFRICA
SENEGAL
PORT GUINEA
SIERRA LEONE
LIBERIA
IVORY COAST
GOLD COAST
DAHOMEY
TOGOLAND
NIGERIA
FRENCH EQUATORIAL AFRICA
ANGLO-EGYPTIAN SUDAN
ERITREA
ABYSSINIA
ITALIAN SOMALILAND
UGANDA
BRITISH EAST AFRICA
CABINDA
BELGIAN CONGO
GERMAN EAST AFRICA
ZANZIBAR
NYASALAND
ANGOLA
NORTHERN RHODESIA
GERMAN SOUTHWEST AFRICA
SOUTHERN RHODESIA
MOZAMBIQUE
MADAGASCAR
BECHUANALAND
UNION OF SOUTH AFRICA

THE TWO WORLD WARS

World War I

World War I (1914–1918) was the most destructive war in world history. Of the 65 million men who served in the different armies, an estimated 10 million died. Large parts of Europe were left in ruins. Some years after the war, in the late 1920s and 1930s, the world was hit by a severe economic crisis. The Great Depression began in the US, before spreading around the world. Thousands of businesses were ruined, and in the US alone 16 million people (a third of the workforce) were out of work. The crisis forced Western governments to reshape their policies. But there was no real improvement in employment until the military aggression of Germany, Italy and Japan created a need for more jobs in the defence and other industries in the 1940s. By then, the world had embarked on another terrible war.

August 1914
Germany invades
Belgium; France, Britain
declare war on Germany

1916
Battles of Verdun
and Somme create
2 million casualties

November 1918
After revolt in Germany,
armistice signed
ending the war

► *Many new weapons made their appearance in World War I. Aircraft were used for the first time. Tanks ended the long stalemate of trench warfare. Poison gas added to the terrors of the battlefield. At sea, no surface vessel, not even the new great battleships, were immune to attack by submarines.*

FURTHER FACTS

● In June 1914 a Serbian terrorist assassinated the heir to the Austrian throne in Sarajevo, Bosnia. Within six weeks Europe was at war – Germany and the Austro–Hungarian empire ranged themselves against France, Britain and Russia.
● The sinking of American merchant ships by German submarines brought the US into the war in 1917. The fresh troops, backed by the resources of the US, caused the final defeat of Germany.

German trench on
Western front

German Fokker triplane

British MK IV tank

Gas mask

UB II German submarine

British battleship HMS *Dreadnought*

WORLD WAR I 1914–1918

Central Powers

Allied Powers

Neutral

NORWAY

SWEDEN

GREAT BRITAIN

London

NETHERLANDS
Brussels
BELGIUM
LUX.

Somme

Paris

Western front

Verdun

Berlin

GERMANY

Brest-Litovsk

Moscow

RUSSIA

Farthest Austro-German penetration

Vienna

AUSTRIA-HUNGARY

SWITZ

FRANCE

Atlantic Ocean

PORTUGAL

SPAIN

ITALY

Rome

Sarajevo

SERBIA

ALBANIA

BULGARIA

GREECE

Gallipoli

Constantinople

OTTOMAN EMPIRE

◄ *World War I changed the map of Europe. In the east, Poland, Latvia, Lithuania and Estonia became independent states. Hungary become a separate republic from Austria. A new state, Czechoslovakia, was created in central Europe. Serbia, Croatia and Slovenia united under a king in an attempt to solve the long-term problems of the Balkan states.*

THE TREATY OF VERSAILLES
The treaty signed in June 1919 ended the war. The British, French and American statesmen who drew it up hoped it would make the world safe from future conflicts. It founded the League of Nations to solve future disputes between states. The League cleared up minor issues but failed to settle major problems. The Germans resented the harsh terms imposed on them and as they recovered from the war they became increasingly hostile towards the League and its members. Once more, Europe became divided into two armed camps.

▲ *Despite its casualties, World War I was fought without a single decisive battle on the Western front. For over four years, fighting centred around two lines of trenches, stretching across western Europe. As the war dragged on, life in the dirty, waterlogged trenches became intolerable for the soldiers who lived in them.*

THE RUSSIAN REVOLUTION
By the end of 1916 the better-equipped Germany army had brought the Russian army near to defeat. In order to reduce Russia to even further chaos, the Germans smuggled the marxist revolutionary Vladimir Lenin (depicted *right* in a 1930s painting) back into Russia from exile abroad. In November 1917 Lenin's Bolshevik (later Communist) party made an attempt to overthrow the Russian government. The troops sent to put down the uprising joined the rioting crowds. Strikes in Petrograd (St Petersburg) grew into a full-scale revolution which saw the downfall of the monarchy and the eventual establishment of a communist dictatorship in Russia.

The Great Depression

After World War I, democratic governments often seemed too weak and indecisive to handle the problems of peacetime, especially the economic crisis of the Depression. Both Italy and Germany became dictatorships under men who promised strong leadership and simple cures for their nation's woes. After a savage civil war, Franco emerged as Spain's leader. The USSR was governed by the tyrannical Joseph Stalin, who forced through a series of ruthless social policies in order to modernize his country.

January 1920
League of Nations'
first meeting

January 1933
Hitler becomes
German Chancellor

September 1939
German army
invades Poland

Queue of
unemployed
in 1930s

PARTITION OF IRELAND

Ireland had been dominated by Britain since the 1100s. At Easter in 1916, British troops crushed a revolt in Dublin by Irish nationalists seeking independence. In 1918 the nationalists declared Ireland an independent state and the Anglo-Irish treaty of 1921, recognized the independence of southern Ireland as the Irish Free State. The six mainly Protestant counties of Ulster remained part of the UK.

◀ *Dublin's post office was at the centre of the 1916 uprising.*

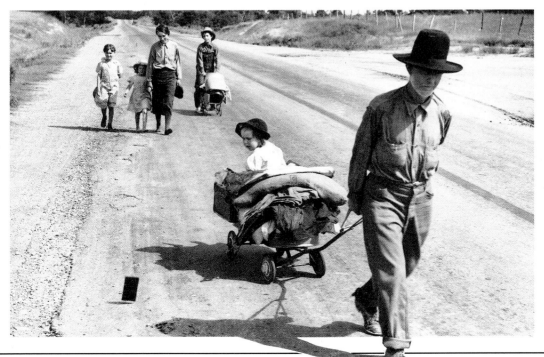

▲ *As world trade declined in the 1930s millions were thrown out of work throughout the West. Banks collapsed, and people lost their savings. The unemployed rioted and everywhere the job queues lengthened. In America, the man-made calamity of the slump was made worse by a natural disaster. In 1934 and 1935, the Midwest was stricken by severe drought. Intensive farming had exhausted the soil and, as the crops died, there was nothing to bind it together. Gales arose and blew the soil away. Thousands of farmers and their families were forced off the land, their livelihoods ruined (left).*

Hitler at Nazi rally

◄ *In Europe the sacrifices of war had been followed by economic suffering. These difficult times provided opportunities for both the German Nazi Party under Adolf Hitler, and Benito Mussolini's Italian Fascist party. Both men came to power promising national recovery. Millions of their fellow-countrymen believed them. Soon both leaders were also seeking territorial expansion in Europe.*

Republican poster in Spanish Civil War

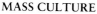

◄ *In 1936, officers of the Spanish army led by General Franco, rebelled against their government. The revolt swiftly developed into a civil war. Foreign states joined in. The fascist (extreme right-wing) powers, Germany and Italy, sent help to the army and its right-wing supporters. Communist Russia aided the government. By 1939 most of Spain had been overrun by the rebels and their leader General Franco was appointed head of state.*

Russian tractors in 1930s

▲ *Lenin died in 1924 and Joseph Stalin succeeded him as head of the USSR. Stalin set out to strip farmers of their land in order to reorganize farming in larger state-owned units called collectives. His orders were brutally carried out by the army and secret police. Villages were burnt and the villagers killed. Millions of people were transported to labour camps in Siberia.*

MASS CULTURE

The new means of communication and travel which appeared between the wars started to break down the old barriers between classes and nations. The first worldwide form of mass culture was the movies. Film actors like the comedian Charlie Chaplin became international idols. In travel, faster aircraft brought the countries of the world closer together, and mass-produced cars increased private travel. In the 1930s, radio and the first television services brought information and entertainment to millions in their own homes.

Charlie Chaplin

Early wireless

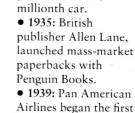
Handley Page HP42 airliner, 1931

Model 'T' Ford

FURTHER FACTS

● **1919:** The German Nazi party and the Italian Fascist party were both founded.
● **1924:** The American Ford motor company produced its ten millionth car.
● **1935:** British publisher Allen Lane, launched mass-market paperbacks with Penguin Books.
● **1939:** Pan American Airlines began the first regular trans-Atlantic air service.

World War II

American *Mustang P51* fighter plane

World War II was an even more destructive war than World War I. Over 50 million people died, the great majority of them innocent civilians. It was caused by the military aggression of three countries – Italy, Germany and Japan (the Axis Powers). At first the Axis won a string of victories. But neither of the three countries had enough resources for a long war. They were eventually defeated by the superior numbers and technology of the Allies – the British Commonwealth, France, USSR and the United States.

German *Tiger Tank*

September 1939
Britain and France declare war on Germany

April 1945
Hitler kills himself; Germany surrenders to Allies in May

August 1945
Japan accepts Allied surrender terms

Japanese battleship *Yomoto*

German V2 rocket

CANADA

UNITED STATES

HAWAIIAN ISLANDS

Pacific Ocean

Atlantic Ocean

GREAT BRITAIN

FRANCE

GERMANY

ITALY

ALGERIA

MOROCCO

LIBYA

FR. WEST AFRICA

EGYPT

ETHIOPIA

Major Allied supply routes

Algeria, French West Africa and Morocco controlled by Axis powers, 1940–1942

USSR Invaded by Germany June 1941
Neutral in war with Japan until August 1945

MANCHURIA

CHINA

JAPAN

INDIA

BURMA

INDOCHINA

PHILIPPINES

NETHERLANDS INDIES

Pacific Ocean

Indian Ocean

AUSTRALIA

NEW ZEALAND

WORLD WAR II 1939–1945

Allied areas   Neutral areas

Axis occupied areas   — Axis expansion

▲ *World War II produced a revolution in armaments. Aircraft with deadlier weapons flew faster and higher. Powerful tanks dominated the battlefield. The aerial strike-power of aircraft carriers made battleships obsolete. German V2 rockets gave a terrifying foretaste of future wars.*

▲ *Both Germany and Japan made huge gains early in the war. Germany dominated the whole of continental Europe. Japan overran the western Pacific and conquered southeast Asia and the East Indies. As the war went on the Russians, Americans, British and their allies regained the lost territories and forced the Axis Powers to surrender.*

▶ *In 1941 the Americans and the Japanese were discussing peace in the Pacific. On 7 December 1941 Japanese planes made a surprise attack on ships of the US fleet based at Pearl Harbor in Hawaii. Within half an hour the US fleet had been crippled. The next day, the US president Franklin D. Roosevelt declared war on Japan and the other Axis Powers.*

THE HOLOCAUST

The most appalling aspect of the Nazi regime was the persecution and extermination of the Jews. Violent attacks on Jews in Germany began in the 1930s and were continued in all the countries the Germans occupied. Death camps were established for the sole purpose of eliminating the entire Jewish population. Altogether, nearly 6 million Jews were murdered.

▶ *Jewish families are herded by German guards onto cattle trucks for transportation to one of several European death camps.*

▶ *In August 1943 Hitler ordered his armies in Russia to capture Stalingrad. By November they had taken most of the city. Then the Russians counter-attacked. Cut off, short of food, and without warm clothing in the Russian winter, the German troops surrendered. The German defeat was a major turning point in the war.*

▼ *By the 1940s bombing raids meant that civilians far from the battlefields had become directly involved in wars. In German air attacks on Britain about 70,000 people died, and about a million Germans died from the Allied bombing raids. A million Japanese civilians were killed by American bombs.*

▼ *In July 1945 America's new president, Harry Truman, gave permission to drop the first atomic bombs on Japan. The bomb that fell on Hiroshima on 6 August killed about 130,000 people. Three days later a second bomb on the city of Nagasaki caused up to 750,000 deaths. The terror the bombs caused persuaded the Japanese to surrender.*

A mushroom cloud forms after the first atom bomb was dropped on Hiroshima

THE POSTWAR WORLD

The Cold War

After the war, world power became divided between two superpowers, the USSR and the United States of America. Instead of disarming, the former wartime partners became rivals in an increasingly dangerous arms race. The result was the so-called 'Cold War', in which a state of hostility existed for decades between the superpowers without actually leading to major conflict. The United Nations, set up at the end of World War II to keep the peace, was powerless to influence the conduct of its two most powerful members. China became communist under Mao Zedong, wars in Korea and Indochina followed, as the USA attempted to contain communist influence in southeast Asia. Superpower rivalry in space technology and travel also led to the race to be first on the Moon, a race won by the USA in 1969.

January 1946 First meeting of the UN General Assembly	**1961** Berlin Wall built as a barrier between East and West	**August 1963** US, USSR and Britain sign nuclear test ban treaty

EUROPE DURING THE COLD WAR
After World War II the wartime co-operation between the USSR and the Western allies collapsed. An 'iron curtain' of mistrust fell between them. By 1950 Europe was cut in two by a string of minefields and border posts which stretched from the Baltic in the north to the Black Sea in the south. In 1949 the Western powers formed a military alliance (North Atlantic Treaty Organization) to fight any Soviet attack.

NATO countries (also includes Canada, USA and Iceland)

Warsaw pact countries

Neutral countries

NORWAY, SWEDEN, FINLAND, IRELAND, UNITED KINGDOM, DENMARK, NETHERLANDS, BELGIUM, LUX., FRANCE, SWITZ, W. GERMANY, E GERMANY, POLAND, CZECHOSLOVAKIA, AUSTRIA, HUNGARY, ROMANIA, YUGOSLAVIA, BULGARIA, ALBANIA, GREECE, ITALY, PORTUGAL, SPAIN, TURKEY, USSR

Allied planes unloading supplies for Berlin, 1949

◀ In 1945, Germany and its former capital Berlin were divided into four Allied occupation zones. In 1948 the Soviets cut all land links between western Germany and the Allied sectors in Berlin. The Allies then airlifted goods into West Berlin. The Soviets allowed the flights to continue in case war broke out. In 1949 Germany split into two states, East and West Germany.

在毛澤東的勝利旗幟下前進

CHINA TURNS COMMUNIST

When the war in Asia and the Pacific ended, a struggle began between the nationalist government under Chiang Kai-shek and the communists led by Mao Zedong (*left*) to decide the future of China. Chiang's forces outnumbered the communists by ten to one but his regime was corrupt and his army poorly trained. His troops deserted in droves and city after city fell to the communists. In 1949 in the capital Peking (Beijing), Mao proclaimed the establishment of the People's Republic of China under communist control.

▼ *The United Nations was founded in 1945 by the wartime Allies. Its purposes are to maintain international peace and to solve problems through international co-operation. Since 1945 the UN's forces have been involved in several conflicts including Korea, the Middle East and Yugoslavia.*

UN Headquarters, New York

◄ *In 1950 North Korea's Soviet-trained army crossed into South Korea. The United Nations condemned the invasion. For the first time, a major international, although mainly American, force gathered under the UN flag. The UN army landed in South Korea and by 1953 North Korea and its Chinese allies were forced to recognize South Korea's independence.*

FURTHER FACTS

● **1948**: Organization for European Economic Cooperation (OEEC) founded. It has since developed into the European Community (EC).
● **1949**: North Atlantic Treaty Organization formed (NATO) – a military alliance between the US and her allies in western Europe.
● **1955**: USSR and her allies sign the Warsaw Pact, an East European defence treaty.

► *Cuba was the centre of a major international crisis in 1962. In 1961 a failed invasion of the island, backed by the USA, confirmed the alliance of Cuba's marxist ruler Fidel Castro with the USSR. During 1962, Soviet nuclear missiles, capable of hitting American cities, were installed in Cuba. US president John Kennedy ordered a naval blockade of Cuba. Nuclear war threatened but the Soviets withdrew their missiles while the US promised not to invade Cuba.*

Missile launchers in Cuba

The World Transformed

The greatest changes of the 1900s have been caused by the dramatic advances in science and technology. New forms of transport, entertainment, household appliances and medical advances are only a few of the areas that have improved the quality of life for most of us. In the past 50 years computers have enabled people to totally transform the world we live in. Used first in business, they are now found in almost every aspect of human life from medicine and education, to home entertainment.

1950s
Elvis Presley begins pop music revolution

1960s
High point of pop art and op art

1980s
Madonna's first album 'Madonna' released

► *In 1957 the USSR launched the first artificial satellite to stay up in space. Soviet scientists followed this success by putting the first person into orbit in April 1961. Americans were humiliated by the USSR's clear lead in space technology. In May 1961 President Kennedy committed the United States to landing an astronaut on the Moon before the end of the decade. Billions of dollars were poured into a US space program. On 20 July 1969, stepping from the lunar module Eagle, US astronaut Neil Armstrong became the first human being to set foot on the Moon.*

▼ *Buying cooked food to be eaten straightaway is not new. Hot pies, jellied eels and roast chestnuts have been sold for centuries. But it has grown enormously in recent decades, with more restaurants selling food that is prepared quickly and easily.*

Fourth landing of American astronauts on the Moon, 1971

▼ *Computers can perform millions of calculations in seconds. They help to design and manufacture many things, including cars, more quickly and cheaply and are becoming increasingly more important in business, education and the home.*

Eating fast food

Personal computer

Communications satellite

Television cameraman

▲ *Satellite television makes it possible to broadcast over vast distances and to several countries at the same time. The first such television broadcast took place in July 1964, when the American satellite Telstar relayed the Olympic Games around the world from Tokyo.*

▶ *Increased pollution is a price we pay for living in the late 1900s. Engine fumes pouring from thousands of vehicles stuck in city traffic jams not only poison human lungs but eat away the fabric of the buildings in which we work and live.*

Traffic jam in American city

FURTHER FACTS

- **1958**: Opening of Guggenheim Museum, New York, designed by Frank Lloyd Wright.
- **1958**: Niemeyer designs the president's palace in Brasília.
- **1985**: Pop singer Bob Geldof organizes 'Live Aid', the famous global pop concert, to help raise money for world famine.

TWENTIETH CENTURY CULTURE

Culture in the late 1900s cannot be readily classified into movements or schools. Much art and music is being produced by young people, for young people. Pop singers such as Elvis Presley, the Beatles and Madonna are transformed by clever promotion and image-making from mere entertainers into role models. American pop artist Roy Lichtenstein used comic strips, advertisements and other common images and made them subjects of art. The American author, Toni Morrison, writes prize-winning books that explore the subject of Black American relationships. New materials and technologies enable architects to design elegant structures of glass and metals. Englishman Henry Moore's sculptures seem to grow naturally from the landscape around them.

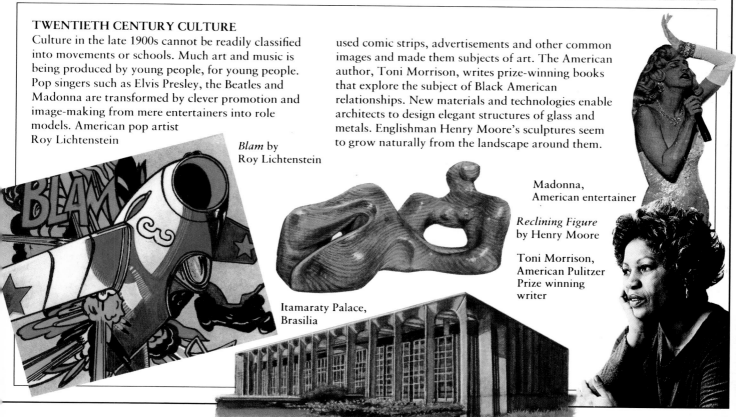

Blam by Roy Lichtenstein

Madonna, American entertainer

Reclining Figure by Henry Moore

Toni Morrison, American Pulitzer Prize winning writer

Itamaraty Palace, Brasília

Retreat from Empire

The old European empires were speedily dismantled in the years following World War II. The effort of fighting the war had weakened the European powers and they became incapable of resisting the various nationalist movements that had grown up in their overseas possessions. India's independence in 1947 began the break-up of the British empire. Between 1950 and 1980 more than 45 former African colonies became independent countries, as well as the majority of Asian and Middle Eastern colonies.

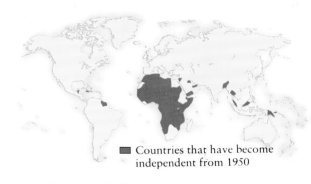

■ Countries that have become independent from 1950

▲ Between 1950 and 1980 most colonies became independent states. The majority were to be found in Africa, south of the Sahara.

1947
India, divided into India and Pakistan, becomes independent

1965–1980
Ruling white minority in Rhodesia (now Zimbabwe) refuses Black majority rule

1954–1975
Wars in Vietnam, involving western powers of France and US

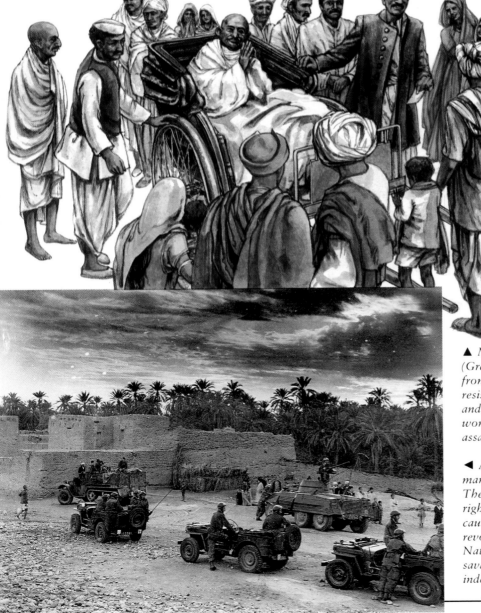

▲ Mohandas Gandhi known as 'Mahatma' (Great Soul) led India to independence from the British. He organized passive resistance to British rule on a mass scale and was imprisoned several times. India won independence in 1947 but Gandhi was assassinated in 1948 by a Hindu fanatic.

◀ Algeria had been French since 1848 and many French colonists had settled there. The refusal of the settlers to grant equal rights to the native Muslim population caused increasing unrest. In 1954 a major revolt led by the Front de Libération Nationale (FLN) resulted in seven years of savage fighting. Algeria became an independent republic in July 1962.

▶ *Vietnam became a united country in April 1975 when the communists of North Vietnam (the Vietcong) captured the southern capital of Saigon from the South Vietnamese and their American allies. Twenty years of war, including some of the heaviest bombing of all time, had devastated the country. As the Vietcong approached Saigon, and the Americans left, many of their South Vietnamese allies tried to flee the country.*

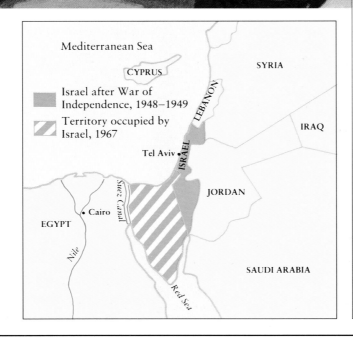

Arab soldiers during 1973 Arab-Israeli war

▲ *In 1947 the UN put forward a plan for separate Jewish and Arab states in the previously British administered territory of Palestine. However, as the British were leaving, the new state of Israel was proclaimed by the Palestine Jews. Since 1947 Israel has fought four wars with her Arab neighbours and Palestine has become divided between Israel, Egypt and Jordan.*

▶ *By the end of the war of 1948–1949 Israel occupied most of Palestine. Gains in the Six Day War (1967) trebled its size. But pressure from the US, and Israel's desire for peace, made it give up most of its gains. Israel signed a peace treaty with Egypt in 1979.*

Mediterranean Sea

CYPRUS

SYRIA

LEBANON

IRAQ

▨ Israel after War of Independence, 1948–1949

▨ Territory occupied by Israel, 1967

Tel Aviv•

ISRAEL

Suez Canal

•Cairo

JORDAN

EGYPT

Nile

SAUDI ARABIA

Red Sea

FURTHER FACTS

● In 1945 the United Nations had 51 members. By 1992 the membership had grown to 179. Most new members had been colonies in the European empires.

● In 1957 Ghana (formerly the Gold Coast) became the first of many countries in Africa to gain independence.

● In the Belgian Congo (now Zaire), Angola and Mozambique there were years of warfare against the colonial power in each country to decide who should run the country after independence.

The New World Order

In the early 1990s the Cold War, which once divided the world into two armed camps, was replaced by conflict between states that had been part of the Soviet empire. Technology, which contines to make rapid advances, usually means a more agreeable life for those who can afford it. Yet pollution of land, sea and air seems to be the penalty for the prosperity of the world's richer nations. Meanwhile, population growth, wars and climatic change have brought severe famine to millions in Africa and Asia.

1960
Sharpeville, South Africa: troops kill 67 black demonstrators

1986
Chernobyl, USSR Nuclear disaster causes international pollution

1992
USSR splits into 15 independent republics

THE FALL OF COMMUNISM

After the war the Soviet Union imposed communism on the countries of eastern Europe that had fallen under its control. Any uprisings against the USSR were ruthlessly crushed. But nationalism in eastern Europe continued. In 1985 a new leader, Mikhail Gorbachev, came to power in the USSR. Gorbachev was committed to reform. He allowed more political freedom within Russia and its subject states. Popular democratic movements sprang up in eastern Europe and led to the overthrow of their communist governments. In 1989 the most hated symbol of communist repression, the wall that divided East and West Berlin, was torn down *(below)*. By 1990 communism in Europe had collapsed.

▼ *Famine, caused by wars and climatic change, means that many millions of people in the world's poorer nations are kept alive only by foreign imported aid of food, medicines and clothing. In Asia, Bangladesh has suffered from catastrophic flooding, while several African countries south of the Sahara Desert are turning into desert wastelands, rife with starvation and disease.*

▼ *Improved farming methods, plants that give higher yields, scientific animal breeding and irrigation schemes have greatly increased the production of food in some developing countries.*

WORLD TRADE ASSOCIATIONS SET UP SINCE 1945

- EFTA
- EC
- COMECON
- ASEAN
- OECD
- **LAIA**
- CACM
- OPEC

▲ *Associations between groups of countries have grown up in many parts of the world. Their objectives vary. Some are merely agreements to cooperate in economic and social matters. The aim of the EC (European Community) is eventually to form complete political union between the nations concerned.*

THE END OF APARTHEID

The apartheid laws passed in 1948 in South Africa separated the population according to race and colour. White people became a privileged ruling class while non-whites were deprived of all civil rights. After 30 years of agitation in South Africa and world-wide condemnation, the apartheid laws began to be dismantled. The respected black leader Nelson Mandela was released after 26 years in prison. In 1991 the apartheid laws were repealed by the government.

Nelson Mandela

FURTHER FACTS

- The first nuclear reactor for generating electricity opened at Obninsk, the USSR in 1954. In 1956 Britain started up the world's first large-scale nuclear power plant, at Calder Hall.
- The General Agreement on Tariffs and Trade (GATT) is an agency set up by the UN. Its purpose is to reduce tariffs and to remove barriers to trade world-wide.

GATT was established in 1958.
- The dismantling of the Berlin Wall was the most dramatic event of the end of the Cold War. On 9 November 1989 East German guards were told to let people pass freely through the checkpoints. The wall, which had stood since 1961, was pickaxed and bulldozed down.

Cleaning up coast after oil slick disaster

▶ *When a fully-laden oil-tanker is wrecked, marine and shore life may be wiped out. Local fishing is destroyed and pollution can remain for many years over a wide area. The risk of such a disaster is considerable, for at any given moment the world's combined tanker fleets are transporting a billion tonnes of crude oil across the high seas. The sinking of the tanker* Braer *off one of the Shetland Isles in northern Scotland in January 1993 has been a catastrophe, both for the people of the islands, and for the sea birds and animals that live there.*

PEOPLE IN WORLD HISTORY

Words in **bold** indicate an entry elsewhere in People in World History and Key Dates in World History.

Akbar the Great (1542–1605): Mogul emperor of India (1556–1605). Conquered most of India. Supported writers and artists and allowed freedom of worship.

Alexander the Great (356–323 BC): King of Macedon and greatest soldier of ancient times. Conquests stretched from Egypt to India; introduced Greek ideas to other lands.

Augustus (63 BC–AD 14): First emperor of Rome (27 BC–AD 14). During his reign Rome was peaceful and prosperous.

Babar (1483–1530): First Mogul emperor. Descendant of **Tamerlane**; invaded northern India; began 200 years of Mogul rule.

Bach, Johann Sebastian (1685–1750): German composer. Wrote concertos, sacred cantatas, clavier works, *St Matthew Passion*, and *B Minor Mass*.

Beethoven, Ludwig van (1770–1827): German composer. Wrote sonatas, symphonies, chamber music, concertos and opera *Fidelio*, considered to be among finest written.

Bismarck, Otto von (1815–1898): German statesman, known as 'the Iron Chancellor'. Was instrumental in uniting Germany under Prussian crown in 1871.

Bolívar, Simón (1783–1830): South American revolutionary leader. Led resistance which freed several South American countries from Spanish rule in early 1800s.

Buddha (Siddhartha Gautama) (*c.* 563–*c.*480 BC): Founder of Buddhism. Son of a wealthy Indian ruler. Left a life of luxury to become a religious leader.

Castro, Fidel (1926–): Cuban marxist and revolutionary. President of Cuba (1959–). Supported revolutions in Africa and Latin America.

Catherine II ('the Great') (1729–1796): Russian empress. German princess, who married future Russian tsar Peter III. Became empress after his murder in 1762. During her reign Russia gained the Crimea and most of Poland.

Charlemagne (*c.* 742–814): King of the Franks and emperor of the West. Empire included Italy, France and most of Germany and Spain. Defended western Europe against Moors, Saxons and Norsemen.

Charles I (1600–1649): King of England (1625–1648). After defeat in Civil War (1642–1648) was tried by a parliamentary court and publicly executed.

Chiang Kai-shek (1887–1975): General and leader of Chinese Nationalist party. President of separate Chinese state of Taiwan (1950).

Churchill, Sir Winston (1874–1965): British statesman, soldier and author. Prime minister (1940–1945 and 1951–1955). Helped maintain British resistance to Nazi Germany. Won Nobel Prize for Literature (1953).

Columbus, Christopher (1451–1506): Italian explorer. 'Discovered' New World (actually Caribbean islands) by accident while seeking route to Asia.

Constantine I ('the Great') (*c.* 274–337): First Christian Roman emperor. Divided Roman empire into East and West. Founded Constantinople as capital of the Eastern empire.

Cook, James (1728–1779): English explorer and navigator. Explored coasts of Australia and New Zealand.

Cortés, Hernán (1485–1547): Spanish conquistador. Conquered Aztec empire and added Mexico to the Spanish empire.

Cromwell, Oliver (1599–1658): English soldier and statesman. General in parliamentary army in English Civil War. Lord Protector (1653–1658).

Eisenhower, Dwight D. (1890–1969): General and 34th president of the USA (1953–1961). Supreme commander of Allied invasion of Europe in World War II (1944).

Elizabeth I (1533–1603): Queen of England (1558–1603). Daughter of **Henry VIII**; reign saw England become important European power; also a golden age of English drama.

Franco, Francisco (1892–1975): Spanish general and statesman. Leader of fascist Falange party; led nationalist rebels to victory in Spanish Civil War (1936–1939). *Caudillo* (ruler) of Spain (1939–1975).

Frederick II ('the Great') (1712–1786): King of Prussia (1740–1786). Made Prussia a leading power in Europe. Patron of writers, philosophers and musicians.

Gama, Vasco da (*c.* 1469–1524): Portuguese navigator and explorer. Led first European expedition to reach India around the Cape of Good Hope (1497–1499).

Gandhi, Mohandas (1869–1948): Indian reformer and political leader, called 'Mahatma' (Great Soul). Led movement for Indian independence and sought to end caste system.

Garibaldi, Giuseppe (1807–1882): Italian freedom fighter and soldier. Leader in struggle (Risorgimento) that united Italy in 1860s.

Genghis Khan (*c.*1167–1227): Mongol leader. Conquered an empire stretching from China to Black Sea.

Gorbachev, Mikhail (1931–): President of USSR (1988–1991). Introduced policies of *glasnost* (openness) and *perestroika* (restructuring). Awarded Nobel Peace Prize (1990).

Hadrian (76–138): Roman emperor (117–138). Ordered building of Hadrian's Wall in northern England as a frontier against invading tribes.

Henry VIII (1491–1547): King of England (1509–1547). Removed English Church from papal control and became supreme head of Church of England. Ordered monasteries to close down and seized their wealth. Married six times.

Hitler, Adolf (1889–1945): German dictator. Founder of National Socialism (Nazi party). German chancellor (1933). Led Germany into war in 1939 by invading Poland. Committed suicide at end of war.

Ho Chi Minh (1890–1969): Vietnamese nationalist leader. Fought French colonial regime (1946–1954). First president of North Vietnam (1954–1969). Led struggle against US-supported South Vietnam.

Jesus Christ (*c.*4 BC–*c.*AD 30): Central figure of Christian religion. A Jew, born in Palestine. After three-year preaching mission, tried and crucified as a political agitator.

Joan of Arc (*c.*1412–1431): National heroine of France. Heard 'voices' telling her to free France from English invaders. After early successes, was captured by the English and burned at the stake as a witch.

Kennedy, John F. (1917–1963): 35th US president (1961–1963). Two major foreign policy crises during presidency were invasion of Cuba (1961) and Cuban Missile Crisis (1962). Assassinated in Dallas, Texas.

Lenin, Vladimir (1870–1924): Russian revolutionary. Founder of Bolshevik (later Communist) party. Led Russian Revolution (1917). Premier and virtual dictator of new communist state.

Leonardo da Vinci (1452–1519): Italian artist and scientist. Considered to be supreme example of Renaissance genius. Paintings include the *Last Supper* fresco and the *Mona Lisa*.

Lincoln, Abraham (1809–1865): 16th US president (1861–1865). Opposed extension of slavery. Led Northern states in American Civil War (1861–1865). Assassinated 1865.

Louis XIV (1638–1715): King of France (164–1715). Known as 'the Sun King'. All-powerful, absolute monarch. Persecutor of French Protestants (Huguenots). Patron of arts; built palace at Versailles.

Luther, Martin (1483–1546): German religious leader. Prime mover in Protestant Reformation.

Magellan, Ferdinand (*c*.1480–1521): Portuguese navigator. Commanded first expedition to sail round the world (1519–1522). Was killed in Philippines on the return journey.

Mandela, Nelson (1918–): Leader of African National Congress in South Africa. Imprisoned 1962–1989. Has since campaigned for democratic, multiracial society.

Mao Zedong or Mao Tse-tung (1893–1976): Chinese Marxist revolutionary leader. Overthrew nationalist government after 20-year struggle. First chairman of Peoples' Republic of China (1949–1976).

Marx, Karl (1818–1863): German philosopher and economist. Co-author (with Friedrich Engels) of *Communist Manifesto* (1848). Exiled to England, wrote *Das Kapital*, key publication of communist philosophy.

Mozart, Wolfgang Amadeus 1756–1791): Austrian composer. Works include more than 40 symphonies, nearly 30 piano concertos, and several operas (*Don Giovanni, The Marriage of Figaro*).

Muhammad (*c*.570–632): Prophet and founder of Islamic faith. His sayings are collected in the Koran. Islam counts its dates from his flight to Yathrib (now Medina) after a plot to murder him (622).

Mussolini, Benito (1883–1945): Leader (*Il Duce*) of Italian fascism. Seized power (1922); allied with Hitler in World War II. Replaced after invasion of Italy by Allies (1943); executed by Italian partisans.

Napoleon I (Bonaparte) (1769–1821): Emperor of France (1804–1814).

Rose to power during French Revolution. After series of military victories, established French empire. Downfall began with invasion of Russia (1812). Final defeat at Waterloo (1815); exiled to St Helena.

Nelson, Horatio (1758–1805): English admiral. Victories during Napoleonic wars kept England safe from invasion; died commanding fleet at Trafalgar (1805).

Peter I ('the Great') (1672–1725): Tsar of Russia (1682–1725). Visited western Europe to study European industrial techniques. Reformed Russian armed forces, government, alphabet and calendar. Built city of St Petersburg as capital.

Philip II (1527–1598): King of Spain (1556–1598), husband of Mary, Catholic queen of England (1554-1558). Strongly anti-Protestant; attempted invasion of England during reign of **Elizabeth I**, Mary's sister, but Armada was defeated (1588).

Pizarro, Francisco (*c*.1478–1541): Spanish conquistador. Conquered Inca empire in Peru with less than 200 men (1532) and killed their emperor, Atahualpa.

Polo, Marco (*c*.1254–*c*.1324): Venetian traveller. Lived at court of Kublai Khan in China. Account of his travels (1271–1295) gave Europeans their first glimpse of life in Asia.

Rembrandt (Harmenszoon van Rijn) (1606–1669): Dutch painter. Greatest achievements are portraits which show deep insight into human character. Works include *The Night Watch, The Anatomy Lesson of Dr Tulp* and self-portraits.

Robespierre, Maximilien (1758–1794): French revolutionary. Lawyer who became leader of Jacobins, most extreme party in French Revolution. Removed rivals during Reign of Terror, but was later arrested and guillotined.

Roosevelt, Franklin Delano (1882–1945): 32nd president of the USA (1933–1945) for a record four terms. His 'New Deal' programme rescued America from Great Depression of 1930s. Co-ordinated Allied war effort after American entry in World War II.

Rubens, Peter Paul (1577–1640): Flemish painter, considered a master of the baroque style. Painted portraits, landscapes, religious and historical subjects.

Saladin (1137–1193): Sultan of Egypt and Muslim warrior. Recaptured Jerusalem and most of Palestine from the Crusaders. Renowned for his military prowess, religious tolerance and justice to his enemies.

Shakespeare, William (1564–1616): English dramatist and poet. Wrote tragedies (*Hamlet*), histories (*Richard III*) and comedies (*Twelfth Night*), generally regarded as among finest plays in the English language.

Stalin, Joseph (1879–1953): Russian communist dictator. Sole ruler of USSR from 1927. Led Russia during World War II. Ruthlessly wiped out any opposition to his rule.

Tamerlane or **Timur** (*c*. 1336–1404): Mongol conqueror and ruler of Turkistan. Seized large parts of central Asia and Near East.

Truman, Harry S (1884–1972): 33rd president of USA (1945–1953). Took decision to drop atomic bomb on Japan (1945). Established NATO (1949). Sent US troops to join UN forces resisting communist invasion of South Korea (1950).

Victoria (1819–1901): Queen of United Kingdom (1837–1901) and empress of India (from 1876). Reigned over British empire at height of its power; gave her name to the period.

Washington, George (1732–1799): General and 1st president of the USA (1789–1797). Commander-in-chief of Continental Army which fought British during American War of Independence (1775–1783).

Wilberforce, William (1759–1833): British statesman and reformer. As Member of Parliament campaigned for abolition of slavery. His Abolition Bill became law in 1807.

Wilhelm II (1859–1941): King of Prussia and emperor of Germany (1888–1918). Ruled personally after dismissing his chancellor **Bismarck** (1890). Abdicated after Germany lost World War I.

William I, 'the Conqueror' (*c*.1027–1087): First Norman king of England (1066–1087). Defeated Saxons under Harold at Hastings (1066). Ordered survey of England which became the Domesday book.

Wilson, Thomas Woodrow (1856–1924): 28th president of the USA (1913–1921). Took America into World War I (1917). After the war, championed League of Nations as means of keeping world peace.

KEY DATES IN WORLD HISTORY

BC

*c.*5 million–1 million: *Homo habilis*, early ancestors of modern humans live in tropical Africa.

*c.*1.5 million: *Homo erectus* learn to make better tools than *Homo habilis*. Move into parts of Europe and Asia.

*c.*9000–8000: First farmers, in the Middle East.

*c.*9000: Tribes of hunters cross from Asia into North America.

*c.*8500: Jericho founded, world's first walled town.

*c.*7000: Pottery produced in Iran.

*c.*5500: Farming begins in Egypt.

*c.*4000–3500: Plough, wheel and sail in use in Mesopotamia and Egypt.

*c.*3500: Mesopotamia: first writing appears in Sumer.

*c.*3000: First evidence of pottery in America.

*c.*2590: Egyptian pharaoh Khufu (or Cheops) builds pyramid at Giza.

*c.*2500–*c.*1628: Minoan civilization in Crete.

*c.*2000: Rise of Babylon.

*c.*2000–1000: Beginnings of Mayan culture in Central America.

*c.*1814–1754: First Assyrian empire.

*c.*1500–600: Hindu religion develops in India.

*c.*1300: Phoenicians develop alphabet to replace picture-writing.

*c.*1200: Beginning of Jewish religion.

776: First Olympic Games in Greece.

753: Legendary founding of Rome.

550: Persian empire founded by Cyrus II; Persia conquers Assyria.

530: Accurate calendar in use in Babylonia.

*c.*500–27: Roman republic.

*c.*480: Death of the **Buddha** (Siddhartha Gautama).

480: Battle of Salamis: Persian invasion of Greece defeated.

*c.*479: Death of Confucius; his teachings became basis of Confucianism.

479–338: Years of Greek civilization's greatest achievements.

336–323: Reign of **Alexander the Great**, king of Macedon.

146: Carthage becomes Roman province of North Africa.

*c.*100: Chinese merchant ships begin trade with India.

54: Roman general Julius Caesar invades Britain.

49: Caesar conquers Gaul (France).

30: Egypt falls to Rome after defeat of Queen Cleopatra at Actium.

27: **Augustus** becomes first Roman emperor – start of Roman empire.

AD

25–222: Han dynasty in China begins great age of Chinese culture.

*c.*30: **Jesus Christ** crucified.

79: Volcano Vesuvius erupts and destroys Pompeii and Herculaneum.

122–127: **Hadrian**'s Wall built as northern frontier of Roman Britain.

135: Palestine becomes Roman province of Judaea.

257: Goths invade Roman empire.

*c.*300: Yamato government established in Japan; Japanese clans practise Shinto religion.

313: **Constantine** ends persecution of Christians in Roman empire.

330: **Constantine** founds Constantinople on site of Byzantium.

391: Emperor Theodosius makes Christianity state religion.

410: Alaric the Goth captures Rome.

433: Attila becomes leader of the Huns.

470: Huns retreat from Europe.

476: End of Western Roman empire.

527–565: Justinian the Great emperor of Eastern Roman (Byzantine) empire.

529: St Benedict founds first Christian monastery, at Monte Cassino, Italy.

*c.*570–*c.*632: Life of **Muhammad**, founder of Islam.

*c.*600: High point of Mayan civilization.

624: Buddhism becomes official religion in China.

*c.*700–1200: Kingdom of Ghana, first West African trading empire.

711: Arabs conquer most of Spain.

732: Battle of Poitiers: Charles Martel checks Arab advance into Europe.

742–814: Life of **Charlemagne**, king of Franks; first Holy Roman emperor.

750: Moors found city of Granada.

*c.*793: First Viking raids in northern Europe.

900: Anasazi begin to build pueblos in southwestern North America.

1000: Viking Leif Ericson lands in North America.

1066: **William of Normandy** invades England; becomes William I.

1071: Muslim Turks stop Christian pilgrimages to Jerusalem.

1086: **William I** orders survey of England (the Domesday Book).

1095: Pope Urban urges Christians to undertake a Crusade to free Holy Land from Muslim rule.

1096: First Crusade begins.

1097: Crusaders capture Jerusalem. Foundation of the Order of Knights Hospitalers.

*c.*1100: Growth of Ife kingdom in Nigeria.

1147–1148: Second Crusade: Crusaders fail to take Damascus.

1187: Saracen leader **Saladin** captures Jerusalem from Christians.

1189–1192: Third Crusade: Crusaders capture Jaffa. Richard I of England signs peace with Saladin.

*c.*1200–1300: Early Inca period in Peru.

1202–1204: Fourth Crusade.

1211: **Genghis Khan** leads Mongols to invade northern China.

1212: Children's Crusade.

1215: English barons force King John to sign Magna Carta, basis of English constitutional practice.

1218: Mongols under **Genghis Khan** overrun Persia.

1234: Mongols overthrow Chin empire in China.

1237: Mongols capture Moscow.

*c.*1250: Berbers establish several states in North Africa.

1260: Kublai Khan becomes ruler of the Mongol Empire.

1264: Kublai Khan founds Yuan dynasty in China.

1275–1292: **Marco Polo** in the service of Kublai Khan in China.

1291: Muslims capture Acre; end of Christian rule in Palestine.

1293: First Christian missionaries in China.

*c.*1300: Rise of Aztecs in Mexico.

*c.*1300: Emergence of Benin empire in Nigeria, West Africa.

1337–1453: Edward III of England claims French throne; Hundred Years' War between England and France.

1347–1351: Black Death comes to Europe from Asia. Millions die.

1352: Ibn Battuta, Berber scholar, recounts visit to Mali in Africa.

1364: Aztecs begin building their capital Tenochtitlán.

1368–1644: Ming dynasty in China; period of stability and prosperity.

1401: **Tamerlane**, ruler of Turkistan, conquers Damascus and Baghdad.

1415: English under King Henry V defeat French at battle of Agincourt.

1429: French led by **Joan of Arc** defeat English at Orléans. Charles VII crowned king of France at Rheims.

1431: **Joan of Arc** burnt by English.

1445: German Johannes Gutenberg publishes *Gutenberg Bible*, first printed book in Europe.

1453: English lose all conquests in France except Calais. Ottoman Turks capture Constantinople; the end of Byzantine empire.

1474: William Caxton prints the first

book in English.

1462–1492: Rule of Lorenzo de Medici in city of Florence; patron of artists such as Michelangelo.

1480: Ivan III, grand prince of Muscovy, frees Russia from Mongols.

1487: Portuguese Bartolomeu Dias first European to round Cape of Good Hope, southern Africa.

1492: Christian Spaniards capture Granada, last stronghold of Moors in Spain. **Columbus** crosses Atlantic and reaches Caribbean islands.

1493: Pope divides New World between Spain and Portugal.

1493–1521: Reign of Huayna Capac, greatest Inca conqueror; founds a capital at Quito, Peru.

1497: Italian John Cabot sails from Bristol, England and reaches Newfoundland in North America.

1498: Vasco da Gama makes first European sea voyage to India.

*c.***1500:** Aztec empire at greatest extent.

1507: The New World named America after Italian navigator Amerigo Vespucci.

1510: Spaniards first import Africans as slaves to work in their American colonies.

1516: Coffee first imported into Europe.

1517: Martin Luther challenges teachings of Catholic Church. Protestant Reformation begins.

1519–1521: Spanish conquistador **Hernán Cortés** conquers Aztec empire in Mexico.

1520–1566: Reign of Suleiman the Magnificent; great age of Ottoman empire.

1526: Babar wins battle of Panipat in India and founds Mogul dynasty.

1531: The Inquisition established in Portugal. Copernicus, Polish astronomer, circulates his theory that the planets move round Sun, not Earth (the Church's teaching).

1532–1534: Francisco Pizarro conquers Inca empire in Peru.

1533–1584: Reign of Ivan IV ('the Terrible'), first tsar of Russia.

1534: English king **Henry VIII** denies authority of the Pope and breaks with Roman Catholic Church. French expedition led by Jacques Cartier reaches Labrador, Canada.

1541: Frenchman John Calvin founds Protestant movement in Geneva.

1545: Council of Trent begins Counter Reformation.

1556–1605: Reign of **Akbar**, greatest of Mogul rulers in India.

1558–1603: Reign of **Elizabeth I** of England; England stays Protestant and becomes major European power.

1562: English start shipping slaves from West Africa to Caribbean.

1571: Turks defeated by alliance of European Christian powers at sea battle of Lepanto. Turkish power in the Mediterranean checked.

1572: Massacre of 20,000 French Protestants on St Bartholomew's Day.

1588: English defeat Spanish Armada.

1598: Edict of Nantes gives French Protestants equal rights with Catholics; ends French Wars of Religion.

1600: British East India Company founded. Tokugawa Ieyasu becomes shogun (ruler) of Japan. His descendants rule Japan for 250 years.

1602: Dutch East India Company founded.

1607: Colony of Jamestown, Virginia founded. The first permanent English settlement in North America.

1608: French traders found Quebec in Canada.

1618–1648: Thirty Years' War between Catholic and Protestant European powers.

1620: Pilgrim Fathers sail from Plymouth, England, in *Mayflower* to Massachusetts in North America.

1637: Japan begins a period of isolation from the rest of the world.

1642–1648: English Civil War.

1643–1715: Reign of **Louis XIV**; France becomes chief European power.

1644: Ming dynasty overthrown; Manchu dynasty founded in China.

1645: Dutchman Abel Tasman first European to reach Tasmania and New Zealand.

1649 King **Charles I** executed; England becomes republic until 1660.

1652: Dutch found colony at Cape of Good Hope (Cape Town).

1658–1707: Rule of Aurangzeb, last of great Mogul emperors.

1663–1699: Ottoman Turks invade central Europe.

1664: English capture New Amsterdam from Dutch. They re-name it New York.

1665: English scientist Isaac Newton discovers gravity.

1670: Hudson's Bay Company founded in England to acquire territory in Canada.

1682–1725: Reign of **Peter the Great** of Russia.

1697–1712: Dominance of Ashanti

empire in West Africa.

1700–1720: Great Northern War between Russia and Sweden.

1701–1714: War of the Spanish Succession; general European war fought over control of Spanish empire after death of Charles II of Spain.

1707: Union of England and Scotland. India: death of Aurangzeb begins decline of Mogul empire.

1733: Founding of Georgia, last of Thirteen Colonies in New England.

*c.***1750s–1850s:** Many new advances in science and technology in Europe sees start of Industrial Revolution.

1756: The Black Hole of Calcutta – British civilians imprisoned by ruler of Bengal die in tiny prison.

1756–1763: Seven Years' War caused by rivalry of Austria and Prussia in Europe, and France and Britain in North America.

1757: British defeat combined French and Indian army at Plassey. Beginning of British supremacy in India.

1757–1843: China limits foreign trade to city of Canton.

1762–1796: Reign of **Catherine the Great** of Russia.

1768–1771: During round the world trip English navigator and explorer **James Cook** reaches Australia and New Zealand.

1775–1783: American War of Independence.

1776: American Declaration of Independence.

1782: Scot James Watt invents rotary steam engine.

1788: Britain sends first convicts to Australia; Sydney is first permanent British settlement.

1789: George Washington becomes the first president of United States of America.

1789–1799: French Revolution.

1793: Execution of Louis XVI; France a republic.

1799: Napoleon becomes first consul and disbands the ruling Directory.

1804: Napoleon crowns himself emperor of France.

1805: British defeat combined Franco-Spanish fleet at Trafalgar.

1807: Slave trade abolished within British empire.

1812: Napoleon's invasion of Russia ends in disaster for him and his army.

1815: British under Wellington and Prussians under Blucher defeat **Napoleon** at battle of Waterloo. **Napoleon** exiled to St Helena.

1818: Shaka forms Zulu nation in southern Africa.

1819: Singapore founded by British as a base for East India Company.

1821–1829: Greek War of Independence against Turkey.

1822: Brazil becomes independent from Portugal. State of Great Columbia (Venezuela, Colombia, Ecuador, and Panama) set up under Simón Bolívar; becomes independent from Spain.

1825: First passenger steam railway opens in England.

1835–1837: Great Trek when Boers leave Cape Colony in South Africa and found the state of Transvaal.

1837–1901: Reign of **Queen Victoria** of Great Britain.

1845: Texas and Florida become states of the USA.

1848: Year of revolutions, including Paris, Milan, Naples, Venice, Rome, Berlin, Vienna, Prague and Budapest. **Marx** and Engels issue *Communist Manifesto*. Californian gold rush.

1853: Gold rush in Australia.

1854: Perry forces Japanese to sign treaty agreeing to trade with USA.

1854–1856: Crimean War; Britain, France and Turkey against Russia.

1857–1858: Indian Mutiny.

1861–1865: American Civil War.

1861: Unification of Italy.

1865: Slavery abolished in USA.

1866: Prussia defeats Austria and wins leadership of Germany.

1867: USA buys Alaska from Russia. Canada becomes British dominion.

1870–1871: Franco-Prussian War.

1871: Germany united; Wilhelm I, king of Prussia, becomes first emperor.

1880–1881: First Boer War between Britain and Dutch settlers (Boers) in Transvaal, South Africa.

1886: Gold discovered in Transvaal; Johannesburg founded.

1890: Wounded Knee, last Native American uprising in USA.

1897: Pierre and Marie Curie discover radioactive element, radium.

1898: Spanish-American war. USA seizes Philippines, Guam and Puerto Rico.

1899–1902: Second Boer War.

1901: Commonwealth of Australia established.

1903: In USA Wright brothers make first powered aircraft flight.

1904–1905: Japan and Russia at war; Japan victorious.

1907: New Zealand becomes British dominion.

1910: Union of South Africa established as British dominion.

1911: Revolution in China. Sun Yat-Sen leads new Chinese republic (1912). Norwegian explorer Roald Amundsen first to reach South Pole.

1912: Henry Ford begins mass production of motor cars in USA.

1914–1918: World War I.

1917: Russian Revolution.

1919: Peace treaty of Versailles signed.

1920: League of Nations founded.

1922: **Mussolini** comes to power in Italy. Irish Free State proclaimed. Union of Soviet Socialist Republics (USSR) founded.

1924: **Lenin** dies; **Stalin** becomes dictator of Russia in 1927.

1927: Charles Lindbergh makes first solo flight across the Atlantic. Civil war in China after Chiang Kai-shek breaks with Chinese communists.

1929: Wall Street crash begins world-wide recession. In India, **Gandhi** begins campaign of civil disobedience against British.

1933: **Hitler** becomes German chancellor; becomes *Führer* (leader) and dictator (1934). US president Roosevelt introduces New Deal policy to end American depression.

1934–1935: **Mao Zedong** leads the Long March of Chinese communists in northern China; establishes him as leader of Chinese communist party.

1935: Nazis begin persecution of Jews in Germany. Italy invades Ethiopia.

1936–1939: Spanish Civil War.

1937: Japanese invade China.

1939: Germany invades Poland.

1939–1945: World War II.

1945: USA drops atom bombs on Hiroshima and Nagasaki. United Nations formed.

1946: Indochina: War between Vietnamese nationalists and French.

1947: India and Pakistan become independent. US aid speeds recovery of Europe (Marshall Plan).

1948: USSR blockades Berlin; the Berlin airlift. State of Israel declared. Arabs at war with Israel.

1949: NATO formed. Germany becomes two republics, East and West. **Mao Zedong** establishes communist rule in China. Apartheid laws introduced in South Africa.

1950–1953: Korean War: N Korea and China against S Korea, the USA and UN troops. US tests hydrogen bomb.

1953: Death of **Stalin**. Tito becomes president of Yugoslavia (until 1980).

1954: French leave Vietnam; Vietnam becomes two states, North (communist) and South.

1954–1962: Algerian war between France and Algerian nationalists.

1955: Communist states in East Europe sign Warsaw Pact.

1956: Britain and France, with Israeli help, fail to take control of Suez Canal, nationalized by Egypt's President Nasser.

1957: Treaty of Rome establishes European Common Market. Ghana (Gold Coast) becomes first British African colony to win independence.

1960: Africa: 17 former French and British colonies become independent.

1961: Berlin Wall built.

1962: Cuban Missile Crisis. Algeria becomes independent from France.

1963: President **Kennedy** assassinated.

1964–1975: Vietnam War: civil war in Vietnam with US forces supporting South Vietnam; ends with victory of communist North Vietnam.

1967: Six Day Arab-Israeli War.

1969: American Neil Armstrong first human on Moon. Violence between Protestant majority and Catholic minority in Northern Ireland (Ulster) brings British troops from mainland.

1971: East Pakistan becomes Bangladesh.

1973: Britain, Denmark and Irish Republic join E.C. Israel defeats Arab states in Yom Kippur war.

1979: Israel and Egypt sign peace treaty. Iran becomes Islamic republic.

1982: Argentina occupies Falkland Islands. Driven out by British troops.

1985–1991: **Mikhail Gorbachev** becomes leader of USSR.

1988: **Gorbachev** begins reforms in USSR – restructuring (*perestroika*) and openness (*glasnost*).

1989: Communist governments in East Germany, Poland, Romania, Bulgaria and Czechoslovakia overthrown by popular uprisings. Dismantling of Berlin Wall.

1990: Unification of Germany. Iraq invades Kuwait.

1991: The Gulf War – UN forces liberate Kuwait. Civil war begins in Yugoslavia. Apartheid laws in South Africa begin to be dismantled. Boris Yeltsin first democratically elected president of Russia.

1992: South African whites vote to negotiate end of white minority rule. Czechoslovakia moves towards separate Czech and Slovak states.

INDEX

Page numbers in *italic* type refer
   to illustrations.
Page numbers in **bold** type refer to
   key topics

A

Aborigines *64*, 65
Acre *26*, *27*, 86
Acropolis *17*
Africa:
   European colonies 68–69
   famines 82, *82*
   independence 80, 81, 88
   slave trade 30, **44–45**, *44–45*, 87, 88
Age of Reason 48–49, *48–49*
   see also Enlightenment
Aircraft *70*, 73, *74*
Akbar, Emperor *38*, 84, 88
Alaric *20*, 86
Alexander the Great 16, 84, 86
Algeria *80*, 88
American Civil War 62–63
American War of Independence 52–53, *52–53*
Americas 30, **34–35**, 37, 40–41, *42*, *42*, 44, 86, 87, 88
   see also North America; South America; United States of America
Amphitheatres *18*
Anasazi *34*, 86
Angola *45*, 81
Apartheid 83, 88
Arabs 24, 25, 44, *81*, 86, 87, 88
Arawaks 37, 40
Archaeologists 10, *10*
Architecture 31, *48*
Armada 33
Armour *21*, *21*, 27, *27*
Army, Roman *20–21*
Art 31, *48*, 78, 79
Arthur, King 23
Asia 38–39
   communism 76
   European colonies 51, 68
   independence 80
   World War II 74
Asoka, Emperor 15
Assyrians *13*, 86
Atahualpa *40*
Athens 16, *17*
Atomic bombs 75, 88
Attila 84, 86
Augustus, Emperor 18, 20, 84, 86
Australia 37, 64, *64*, 65, 87, 88
Australopithecines *10*
Austria 70, *71*
Axis Powers 74
Aztecs 34, *34*, *40*, 86, 87

B

Babar *38*, 84, 87
Babylonians *13*, 86
Bach, Johann Sebastian *49*, 84
Bahamas 34, 36
Balkans 38, *71*
Ballet 48, *48*
Bangladesh 82, 88
Baroque art *48*, 85
Bastille *54*, 55
Baths, Roman *19*
Bayeux Tapestry *23*
Beatles 79
Beethoven, Ludwig van 84
Beijing 39, 69, 77
Belgian Congo (now Zaire) 81
Belgium 59, 60, 61, 70
Bengal *51*
Benin empire *44*, 86
Berlin Wall 76, 82, 83, 88
Bible, The 15
Bismarck, Otto von 84
Black Death 28–29, *29*, 86
Black Hole of Calcutta 51
Boleyn, Anne 33
Bolívar, Simón 61, 84
Bolivia 61
Boston Tea Party 52
Bows and arrows 28, 35
Boyars *46*
Brazil 40, 45, *51*, 88
Britain:
   British empire 41, 50, 68–9, *68*, 80, *80*
      Civil War 46, 47, 87
      Hundred Years' War 28
      Industrial Revolution 58–59, *58–59*
      Napoleonic wars 56, 57
      nuclear power 83
      Reformation in *32*, 33
      slave trade *45*
      theatres 42, *43*
      World War I 70
      World War II 74, *74–75*
Britain, Battle of 75
Bruegel, Peter 31
Brunelleschi, Filippo 31
Buddhism 14, 15, *15*, 84, 86
Bunker Hill, battle of 53
Byzantine empire 21, 38, 86, 87

C

Cabot, John 37, 87
Cabral, Pedro 40
California 65
Calvin, John 32, 33, 87
Canada 41, 65, 87, 88
Canals 58
Cape of Good Hope 40, *50*, 87
Caravels *36*

Carpaccio, Vittore 31, *31*
Carthaginians 18
Castles 26, 28
Castro, Fidel 77, 84
Catherine of Aragon 33
Catherine the Great 84, 87
Catholic Church 32–33, 39, 49, 69
Cave paintings *11*
Caxton, William 31, 87
Centurion, HMS 51
Champlain, Samuel de *50*
Chaplin, Charlie 73, *73*
Charlemagne 84, 86
Charles I, king of England 46, 47, 84, 87
Charles II, king of England *44*, 46, 49
Charles VII, king of France 28
Charles X, king of France 61
Chernobyl 82
Chiang Kai-shek 77, 84
Child labour 59
Chile 61
China 38–39, 86, 88
   communism in 76, 77, 88
   Marco Polo visits 37, 38
   Han dynasty 86
   Ming dynasty 39
   Opium wars 69
   religions 14, 15, *15*, 86
Chivalry 27
Christianity *14*, **24**
   Crusades 26–27
   in Middle Ages 22
   missionaries 49, 69
   Reformation **32–33**, 87
   in Roman empire 21, 86
   Victorian Age 66
Church of England 33
Churchill, Sir Winston 84
Circus Maximus 18, *18*

Cistercians *24*
Clocks, early *31*
Clouet, François 31
Coats of arms 27
Colbert, Jean Baptiste *47*
Cold War 76–77, *76–77,* 82, 83
Colonies 50–51, *50–51,* **68–69,** *68–69,*
    80–81, *80–81*
Columbia 61
Columbus, Christopher 34, 36, 37,
    37, 40, 84, 87
Commonwealth 74
Communism 61, 71, 76, 77, 82, 88
Compasses 36
Computers 78, *78*
Confederate States 62, 63
Confucianism *14,* 15
Confucius *15,* 86
Conquistadors 34, 40
Constantine I, Emperor *21,* 84, 86
Constantinople 20, 38, 86
Convicts (in Australia) 64, *64,* 65
Cook, Captain James 36, *37,* 84, 87
Córdoba 25
Cortés, Hernán 40, *40,* 84, 87
Cort, Henry 58
Cotton *42*
Counter Reformation 32–33
Covadonga 51
Crete 16, 17
Cromwell, Oliver 46, *47,* 84
Crusades 26–27, 86
Cuba 77, 88
Culture, 20th-century 79
Cuneiform writing 12, 13, 86
Czechoslovakia *71,* 81, 88

D

Darius, king of Persia 16, *16*
Dating, radiocarbon 10
Davis, Jefferson *62*
Dawson, Canada 65
Declaration of Independence 52, *53,* 87
Dekker, Thomas 43
Delhi *68, 68*
Democracy 16

Department stores 67, *67*
Descartes, René 48, 49
Dias, Bartolomeu 37, 87
Diderot, Denis 48, 49, *49*
Dome of the Rock, Jerusalem 25
Domesday Book 23, *23,* 86
Dublin 72, *72*
Dürer, Albrecht 31

E

East India Companies 50, 51, 52, 87, 88
East Indies *50,* 51, *51,* 68, *74*
Ecuador 61
Egypt 12–13, *12–13, 81,* 86, 88
Eisenhower, Dwight D. 84
Elizabeth I, Queen *33,* 43, 84, 87
Ellis Island 65
El Mina 45
Encyclopédie 48, 49, *49*
England *see* Britain
Enlightenment 48–49, *48–49*
    see also Age of Reason
Erasmus *30,* 31
Estonia *71*
Etruscans 18
Euphrates Valley 12
European Community (EC) 77, *83*
Explorers 36–37
Eyck, Jan van 31
Eylau, battle of *57*

F

Factories 58–59
Famines 65, 82, *82*
Farming *11,* 43, *43, 59, 82,* 86
Fascist parties 73, *73*
Flags, American Civil War *62*
Florence 30, 31, *31,* 87
Food (tastes in) *42, 78,* 87
Ford Motor Company 73, 88

Forum, Roman *19*
France 86, 87, 88
    colonies 41, 50, 68, 69, *69,* **80**
    Franco-Prussian War *61*
    Hundred Years' War 28
    Napoleon Bonaparte **56–57,** *56–57*
    Renaissance *30*
    under Louis XIV 46, 47, *47,* 84, 87
    World War I 70, *71*
    World War II *74,* 75
Franco, General 72, *73,* 84
Frederick II the Great, king of
    Prussia 48, *49,* 84
French Revolution 52, **54–55,** *54–55,*
    60, 61, 87

G

Galileo 31
Gama, Vasco da 37, *37,* 84, 87
Gandhi, Mahatma *80,* 84, 88
Garibaldi, Giuseppe *60,* 84
GATT (General Agreement on Tariffs
    and Trade) 83
Gautama 15
Geldof, Bob 79
Geneva 32, 33, 87
Genghis Khan 22, *23, 28,* 84, 86
Germany:
    Cold War 76
    colonies 68
    emigration to America 64
    Franco-Prussian war *61,* 88
    Napoleonic wars 56
    Nazis 72, 73, *73,* 88
    unification 60, 88
    World War I 70–71
    World War II 74–75, *74–75,* 88
Gettysburg, battle of 63
Ghana (Gold Coast) 45, *81,* 86, 88
Giza *12*
Gladiators 19, *19*
Globe theatre, London 43
Gobelins tapestries *47*
Gods, Greek 15
Gold Coast (Ghana) *45,* 81
Gold rushes 65, 88
Gorbachev, Mikhail 82, 84, 88
Great Depression 70, 72–73, *72–73*
Great Zimbabwe 44
El Greco 31
Greece 16–17, *60, 60,* 86, 88
Greenwich Observatory *49*
Gregory, Pope 42
Guggenheim Museum, New York 79
Guinea *44*
Gutenberg, Johannes 31, *31,* 86

H

Hades *17*
Hadrian, Emperor 84, 86
Hargreaves, James 59
Harold II, King of England 23, *23*
Hastings, battle of 23, *23*
Hawaii *37, 74*
Hebrews *14*
Henry VIII, king of England 32, 33,
    33, 84, 87
Heraldry *27*
Hieroglyphics *12*
Hinduism 14, *14*, 15, *15*, 38
Hiroshima 75, 88
Hispaniola 36, 37, 40
Hitler, Adolf 72, *73, 75, 75*, 84, 88
Ho Chi Minh 84
Holbein, Hans 31
Holocaust 75
Holy Land 26–27, *26–27*, 86
Horse races 19, *19*
Huang He Valley *12*
Hudson's Bay Company 41, 87
Hudson Valley *50*
Humanism *30*
Hundred Years' War 28, 86
Hungary 71

I

Ibn Battuta 37, 86
Ife *44*, 86
Incas 34, *34, 40*, 86, 87
India:
    British rule *51*, 68, *68*, 87
    independence 80, *80*, 88
    Mogul empire 38, *38*, 46, 87
    religions 14, *14*, 15, 86
Indian Mutiny 68, 88
Indochina 69, 76, 88
Indonesia 51
Industrial Revolution 58–59, *58–59*, 68
Indus Valley *12*
Inquisition *33*, 87
Inventions 67
Ireland 46, 64, 65, 72, 88
Iron Curtain 76
Iroquois tribes *35*
Islam *14*, 22, **24–25**, 86, 88
    in Africa *45*
    in Algeria *80*
    Crusades 26–27
    Ottoman empire 38
    Spanish Inquisition *33*
Israel *81*, 88
Israelites *14*

Italy:
    emigration to America 64
    fascists 72, 73, *73*
    Renaissance 30
    Risorgimento 60, *60*, 88
    World War II 74

J

Jacobins 55
Japan 15, 38, *39*, 49, *68*, 74, *74–75*, 86,
    87, 88
Jefferson, Thomas 52
Jerusalem *14*, 25, 26, 27, 86
Jesus Christ 24, 26, 84, 86
Jews 14, 15, 24, *33*, 75, *75, 81*, 86, 88
Joan of Arc 28, 84, 86
Johnson, Dr Samuel 49
Josephine, Empress 56
Judaism *14*, 15, 24

K

Kennedy, President John 77, 84, 88
Kings 46–47, *46–47*
Knights 27, *27*
Knights Hospitalers *26*, 86
Knights Templars *26*
Korea 76, 77, 88
Krak des Chevaliers *26*
Kristina, queen of Sweden 49
Kublai Khan 38, 86
Kyoto *39*

L

Lamarck, Jean-Baptiste *48*
Lane, Allen 73
Lao-Tzu *15*

Latvia *71*
League of Nations 71, 72, 88
Lenin, Vladimir 71, *71, 73*, 85, 88
Leonardo da Vinci *31*, 85
Lichtenstein, Roy 79
Lincoln, Abraham 62, *62*, 85
Linnaeus *48*
Lithuania *71*
Livingstone, Dr David 69
London 43
Louis XIV, king of France 46, 47, *47*,
    85, 87
Louis XVI, king of France *54*, 55, 87
Louis Philippe, king of France 61
Luther, Martin 32, *32, 33*, 85, 87

M

Madonna 78, 79, *79*
Magellan, Ferdinand 37, *37*, 85
Manchester 59
Mandela, Nelson 83, 88
Manhattan Island *50*
Mao Zedong (Mao Tse-tung) 76, 77, *77*,
    85, 88
Marie Antoinette, queen of France *54*,
    55
Marlowe, Christopher 43
Marx, Karl 61, *61*, 85, 88
Mayan civilization 34, *34*, 86
Medici family 30, 31, 87
Mediterranean *13*, 16, 18, 87
Mexico 40, *40*, 51, 61, 87
Michelangelo 31, 87
Middle Ages 22–29
Middle East *11, 14*, 77, 80
Middleton, Thomas 43
Migration 64–65, *64–65*
Ming dynasty 38, *39*, 86, 87
Minoans 16, 17, 86
Missionaries 39, 49, 69
Mogul empire 38, *38*, 46
Mohawk tribe *35*
Monasteries 24–25, 29
Mongols 23, 28, 86
Montezuma *40*
Moon landings 76, 78
Moore, Henry 79
Moors *25*, 86, 87
More, Sir Thomas 31
Morrison, Toni 79, *79*
Moscow 57
Mozambique 81
Mozart, Wolfgang Amadeus 85
Muhammad, Prophet 24, 25, *25*, 85, 86
Muslims *see* Islam
Mussolini, Benito 73, 85, 88

N

Nagasaki 39, 75, 88
Napoleon Bonaparte 54, **56–57**, *56–57*, 60, 85, 87–88
Nationalism 60–61, 80, 82
Native Americans 35, 40, 41, *50*, 63, 88
NATO (North Atlantic Treaty Organization) 76, 77, 88
Nazi party 73, *73*, 75, 88
Nelson, Horatio 56, 57, 85
Netherlands 50, *51*, 68
New England 40, *41*
New South Wales *64*
Newton, Isaac 42, *42*, 87
New World Order 82–83, *82–83*
New York 50, *53*, 65, 79, 87
New York State *35*
New Zealand *37*, 64, 87, 88
Nicot, Jean *42*
Niemeyer, Oscar 79
Nile Valley 12–13
Normans 23, *23*
North America 34, 41, 48, *50*, 86
see also United States of America
Nuclear power 82, 83
Nuclear weapons 75, 76, 77, 88

O

Odo, Bishop *23*
Orellana, Francisco de 40
Oil pollution *83*
Olmecs 34
Olympic Games *17*, 79
Opera 48, *48*
Ottoman empire 38, 60, 86, 87, 88

P

Pacific Ocean 36, *37*, 68, *74*
Paintings, cave *11*
Pakistan 80, 88
Palestine *14*, 24, 26, *81*, 86
Pan American Airlines 73
Paris *32*, 55, *61*, 88
Parthenon *17*
Pasteur, Louis 67
Pearl Harbor *74*
Peasants 28, *43*
Peking *see* Beijing
Penguin Books 73
Perry, Commodore Matthew 68, 88
Persephone *17*
Persians *13*, 16, *16*, 86
Peru *34*, 40, *40*, 87
Peter the Great 46, *46*, 85, 87
Philip II, king of Spain *33*, 85
Philippines 68
Pilgrimages 26, 27
Pilgrim Fathers *41*
Pizarro, Francisco 40, *40*, 85, 87
Plague 28–29, *29*, 43
Plassey, battle of *51*
Poitiers, battle of 24
Poland 57, 61, *71*, 72, 88
Pollution 79, 82, *83*
Polo, Marco 36, 37, *37*, 38, 85, 86
Pompeii *18*, *19*, *19*, 86
Portugal *36*, 40, 45, *50*, *51*, 60, 68, 87
Potatoes *42*, 65
Prehistoric people 10–11
Presley, Elvis 78, 79
Printing 30, *31*
Protestant Churches 32–33
Prussia 48, 49, 60, *61*
Punic wars 18
Puritans 33
Pyramids *12*, 34

Q

Quebec *50*, 87

R

Rabelais, François 31
Races, horse 19, *19*
Radiocarbon dating 10
Railways 59, *59*, 62, 63, *63*, 88
Raleigh, Sir Walter 31
Rats, plague 29, *29*
Reformation 30, **32–33**

Religions **14–15**
Reformation and Counter Reformation **32–33**, 87
Roman *19*
Vikings *22*
see also individual religions
Rembrandt *43*, 85
Renaissance 22, **30–31**
Revolutions 52–55, 58–61, 71
Rhodesia (Zimbabwe) 80
Richard I, king of England 26, 86
Risorgimento 60
Roads, Roman 19, 20
Robespierre, Maximilien 54, 55, *55*, 85
Roman empire 18–21, 86
Rome 31, 60, 88
Romulus and Remus 18, *18*
Romulus Augustus, Emperor 20
Ronsard, Pierre de 31
Roosevelt, Franklin 74, 85, 88
Rosetta stone 12, *12*
Rubens, Peter Paul 48, 85
Russia 46, *46*, 56, 57, *60*, 64, 87, 88
see also USSR
Russian revolution 71

S

St Bartholomew's Day massacre *32*, 87
St Helena *57*, 88
St Petersburg *46*, 71
Saladin 26, 85, 86
Samarkand 28
San Francisco 65
San Martín, José 61
Santorini *17*
Saracens 26
Saratoga, battle of 52
Sargon 12

Satellites 78, 79
Science and technology 42, 78–79, 78–79, 82
Scramble for Africa 68
Seljuk Turks 26
Senate, Roman 20
Serfs 46
Servants, Victorian Age 66, 66
Seven Years' War 50, 50
Shakespeare, William 42, 43, 43, 85
Shanghai 69
Sharpeville massacre 82
Shetland Isles 83
Shinto 15
Ships:
　caravels 36
　Egyptian 13, 13
　slave trade 45
　Viking 22, 22
Shops:
　department stores 67, 67
　Roman 18
Siam (now Thailand) 51, 68, 69
Siberia 61, 73
Siena 31
Sioux tribes 35
Six Day War 81
Slavery 30, 44–45, 44–45, 62, 62, 85, 87, 88
Snofru, Pharaoh 13
Solomon, King of Israel 14
Somme, battle of the 70
South Africa 50, 82, 83, 88
South America 34, 40, 42, 60, 61, 64
Spain:
　Civil War 72, 73, 88
　colonies 51, 60, 68, 87
　conquistadors 36, 40, 50
　Moors in 25
Spanish Armada 33, 87
Sparta 17
Sri Lanka 15
Stalingrad 75
Stalin, Joseph 72, 73, 85, 88
Stanley, H.M. 69
Stephenson, George and Robert 59
Street vendors 67
Submarines 70
Suleiman the Magnificent 38, 87
Sumer 12, 86
Sydney 64
Syria 17, 26

Tea 39, 43, 52
Technology 78–79, 78–79, 82
Telescopes 42
Television 79
Tennis Court Oath 54, 55
Tenochtitlán 40, 86
Terror, Reign of 54, 55
Testudo, Roman 21
Thailand see Siam
Theatres 17, 18, 42, 43, 43
Theodosius, Emperor 20, 21, 86
Tigris Valley 12
Timur (Tamerlane) 28, 85, 86
Tipu Sultan 51
Tobacco 42, 43
Tokyo 68, 79
Tombs, Egyptian 12–13
Tournaments 27, 27
Trafalgar, battle of 56, 56, 57, 87
Trent, Council of 32, 33, 87
Truman, Harry 75, 85
Tull, Jethro 59
Turkey 38, 60, 88

U
Ulster 72, 88
United Nations 76, 77, 81, 81, 83, 88
United States of America:
　Civil War **62–63**, 88
　Cold War **76–77**, 88
　colonies 68, 87
　Declaration of Independence 52, 53, 87
　Great Depression 70, 72
　immigration 41, **64–65**, 64–65, 87, 88
　Moon landings 78, 69, 88
　Vietnam war 81, 88
　World War I 70
　World War II 74, 74–75,
Urban II, Pope 26
USSR 88
　Cold War **76–77**
　collapse of 82
　nuclear power 82, 83
　satellites 78

Stalin 72, 73, 88
World War II 74, 75
see also Russia

V
Venice 31, 88
Verdun, battle of 70
Versailles, palace of 47, 47
Versailles, treaty of 71
Vesalius, Andreas 43
Vespucci, Amerigo 37, 37, 87
Victorian Age 66–67, 66–67
Victoria, Queen 66, 85, 88
Vienna 38, 38, 88
Vietnam 68, 69, 80, 81, 88
Vikings 22, 22, 23, 86
Villas, Roman 19
Visigoths 20
Voltaire 49

W
Warsaw Pact 77, 88
Washington, George 53, 53, 85, 87
Waterloo, battle of 56, 57, 57, 88
Weaving 59
West Indies 36
Wilberforce, William 85
Wilhelm I, emperor of Germany 61, 84
Wilhelm II, emperor of Germany 85
William the Conqueror 22, 23, 85, 86
Wilson, President Woodrow 85
Wolfe, General James 50
World War I 70–71, 70–71, 72, 88
World War II 74–75, 74–75, 88
Wright, Frank Lloyd 79
Writing 12, 13, 17

Y
Yahweh 14, 15
Yorktown, battle of 53, 53
Yugoslavia 71, 77, 88
Yukon 65

T
Tanks 70, 74
Taoism 14, 15, 15
Tasmania 65, 87

Z
Zaire (Belgian Congo) 81
Zanzibar 45
Zimbabwe (Rhodesia) 44, 80

The publishers would like to thank the following artists
for contributing to the book:

Jonathan Adams 47, 54, 58–59, 61, 72–73, 77;
Marion Appleton 10–11, 12, 15, 18–19, 21, 22–23, 25, 27, 29, 31, 34, 36, 38–39, 44, 47, 48–49, 59, 79, 83;
Vanessa Card 24; Dean Entwistle 12–13, 18–19, 24–25; Eugene Fleury maps, various pages;
Mark Franklin maps, various pages; Terry Gabbey (EVA Morris AFA) 10–11,
14–15, 31;
Peter Gregory 35, 78–79, 80; Andre Hrydziusko (Simon Girling) 26, 31;
Simon Huson 10;
Ron Jobson (Kathy Jakeman Illustration) 22, 27, 33, 36, 59, 67, 74;
Kevin Jones Associates 32, 35, 39, 40, 45, 59, 73, 76–77;
Peter Kestervan (Garden Studio) 19, 24, 36, 62–63, 70–71;
Deborah Kindred (Simon Girling) 23, 25, 29, 30, 41;
Mike Lacey (Simon Girling) 28, 56–57, 72; Jason Lewis 43; Chris Lyon 75;
Louis Mackay (Linda Rogers) 30, 42;
Dave McAllister (Simon Girling) 13, 20–21, 26–27, 40–41, 52–53, 68–69;
Tony Morris (Linda Rogers) 49, 54, 65, 78; Trevor Parkin (Linda Rogers) 43, 45;
Mike Roffe 51; Martin Salisbury (Linda Rogers) 43, 60, 73, 79, 83;
Rodney Shackell 33, 43, 45, 48–49, 55, 60–61, 62, 64, 67; Rob Shone 25, 66;
Nick Shewring 73; Paul Stangroom 30, 32–33, 55, 60, 62, 82;
Roger Stewart 50–51, 54, 66, 67; Graham Sumner (Simon Girling) 46–47, 52–53, 64, 80;
Mike Taylor 59

The publishers would like to thank the following for supplying
photographs for this book:

Frontispiece AKG; page 16–17 SCALA; 18 AKG; 23 Permission of Town of Bayeux;
25 ZEFA; 27 British Museum; 28 British Library (top), Bridgeman Art Library
(bottom); 31 AKG; 34 British Museum; 35 British Museum; 38 AKG; 39 British
Museum; 42 Science Museum; 43 Bridgeman Art Library; 48 AKG; 52 Peter Newark
Pictures (left), Library of Congress (right); 53 Peter Newark Pictures; 57
Bridgeman Art Library; 63 AKG; 65 Mary Evans Picture Library (left),
Bettmann Archive (right); 68 Bridgeman Art Library; 69 National Army Museum;
71 AKG; 72 Bettmann Archive; 74 Imperial War Museum; 75 Wiener Library/Beate
Klarsfeld Foundation (top), Associated Press (middle), Imperial War Museum
(bottom); 77 Popperfoto; 79 Popperfoto (middle), Chatto and Windus (bottom);
80 Hulton-Deutsch Collection; 81 Popperfoto; 82 Frank Spooner Pictures.

(AKG = Archiv Fur Kunst Und Geschichte)